INTERMEDIATE LOAN

THIS ITEM MAY BE BORROWED FOR
ONE WEEK ONLY

Intermediate loans are in heavy demand. Please return or renew.
To renew, telephone :
01243 816089 (Bishop Otter)
01243 816099 (Bognor Regis)

Racism in children's lives

Both teachers and the general public have traditionally been unwilling to acknowledge that concepts of 'race' might play a part in the lives of primary school children. For this book Barry Troyna and Richard Hatcher spent a term in each of three mainly white primary schools, talking to pupils in their last two years of primary education. They talked to black and white pupils individually and in small groups outside the classroom about issues, not necessarily of 'race', which the children themselves saw as important. From these conversations they built up a fascinating study of how 'race' emerges for young children as a plausible explanatory framework for incidents in their everyday lives and the primary school world. The final picture is both disturbing in its demonstration of how significant racism is in the lives of white children and hopeful in showing how frequently anti-racist attitudes exist even in the thinking of children who engage in racist behaviour. A final chapter looks at how school policy can combat racism and build on these positive elements.

Barry Troyna is a Senior Lecturer in Education at the University of Warwick. He has been involved in anti-racist education for over fifteen years as a teacher, campaigner, lecturer and governor. **Richard Hatcher** is Senior Lecturer in Educational Studies at Birmingham Polytechnic. He has been concerned with issues of 'race' and education for many years, as a teacher, lecturer, school governor and within the Labour Party.

Racism in children's lives

A study of mainly-white primary schools

Barry Troyna
and
Richard Hatcher

ROUTLEDGE in association with the National
Children's Bureau

First published 1992
by Routledge
11 New Fetter Lane, London EC4P 4EE

Simultaneously published in the USA and Canada
by Routledge
a division of Routledge, Chapman and Hall, Inc.
29 West 35th Street, New York, NY 10001

© 1992 Barry Troyna and Richard Hatcher

Typeset in Baskerville by Selectmove Limited.
Printed and bound in Great Britain by
Biddles Ltd, Guildford and King's Lynn

British Library Cataloguing in Publication Data
Troyna, Barry
    Racism in children's lives : a study of mainly-
    white primary schools.
    I. Title   II. Hatcher, Richard
    370.19342

    ISBN 0–415–06085–0
    ISBN 0–415–06086–9 pbk

Library of Congress Cataloguing in Publication Data
Troyna, Barry
    Racism in children's lives : a study of mainly-white
    primary schools / Barry Troyna and Richard Hatcher.
    Includes bibliographical references and index.
    ISBN 0–415–06085–0. – ISBN 0–415–06086–9
    1. Discrimination in education–Great Britain.   2. Minorities-
    Education (Elementary)–Great Britain.   3. Racism–Great Britain.
    4. Great Britain–Race relations.   I. Hatcher, Richard, 1944–
    II. Title
    LC212.3.G7T76   1992
    370.19′342–dc20   91–28464
                                                              CIP

During the course of this research four outstanding and active anti-racist educationists passed away: Ann-Marie Davies, Paul Hibbert, Keith Kimberley and David Ruddell. We'd like to acknowledge their innovative and inspirational contribution to the development of anti-racist education.

Barry Troyna and
Richard Hatcher

Contents

Figures and tables

Acknowledgements

The research reported in this book was made possible by a grant awarded by the Economic and Social Research Council (reference X204252006) to Barry Troyna and David Berridge which enabled the appointment of Richard Hatcher to carry out the discussions with the children. Sue Tall was the administrative secretary and did a splendid job in transcribing over 150 hours of interview material. Thanks also to Les Back, David Berridge, Maud Blair, Bob Burgess and Martyn Denscombe for reading and commenting on initial drafts of the book and to the specialist advisers in 'Greenshire' and 'Woodshire' for arranging access to schools in their areas. Above all, we would like to express our gratitude to the headteachers of the three schools; to the teachers whose unstinting cooperation made the research possible, and especially the children for allowing us to discuss with them such personal and important issues. We hope we have done them justice.

We'd like to thank the executive editors of the *Journal of Education Policy* for their permission to reproduce sections of our article, 'Racist Incidents in Schools: a Framework for Analysis'.

Barry Troyna would like to say thanks to Pat Sikes, Julia Stanley and Carol Vincent for making his study leave feasible; Margaret Handy, Sue Tall and Donna Jay for their superb secretarial support; and to Pat, Jayne, Chris, Donna and John for their general backing and encouragement. Richard Hatcher would like to say thanks to Elaine.

Chapter 1

Introduction

'RACIST' screamed the front page headline of the *Newcastle Evening Chronicle* in March 1907. And the news item? The decision of a local primary school headteacher to designate a white child's refusal to hold hands with a black school mate as a 'racial' incident and report it to the local council offices. The headteacher's action was in line with the City Council's policy on racial equality and its guidelines to all schools on how to monitor 'racial' incidents. But the headteacher's action provoked a hostile response from local Conservative councillor Mike Summerby who insisted that 'the whole thing appears to be ludicrous'. As he put it to the paper's Municipal Editor, Peter Young:

> I was aware we require headteachers to report any racial incidents at their schools, which seems to be perfectly reasonable.
>
> I have taken this to mean hard evidence of racial prejudice or maybe, the National Front standing outside a school with leaflets.
>
> But to suggest there is anything racial in a primary school pupil refusing to hold hands with another primary school pupil is ridiculous.
>
> (13 March 1987, p. 1)

Councillor Summerby's outrage at the headteacher's alleged inflation of what constitutes a 'racial' incident and his reluctance to accept that children of primary school age might participate in such activities are not uncommon. Nor is the status conferred on the item by the *Evening Chronicle*. In 1988, for instance, 'RACIST CHECK ON TODDLERS' was emblazoned across the front page of the *Daily Mail*: a critical response to the publication of Hertfordshire County Council's initiative to tackle racism in all its educational institutions. This was followed, a week later, by an article and editorial in the *Mail* denouncing the nature of the research reported in this book. Under the heading, 'Big brother and tiny tots' the *Mail* editorial informed its readers that this 'galumping project . . . sounds about as sensible as unleashing a bloodhound in a doll's house' (11 October 1988, p. 6).

The thrust and tenor of these headlines and articles resonate with the central themes of this book. To begin with they articulate the widespread reluctance of professional teachers and laypersons to accept that 'race' might shape and constrain young children's lives. The availability of an impressive array of empirical research on this matter, drawn from an equally impressive range of methodologies and settings, continues to sit uneasily with commonsense assumptions about children and an idealised conception of the world in which they reside. 'They're too Young to Notice', the deliberately ironic title of Ian Menter's (1989) review of research on young children and racism is testimony to how widespread and tenacious are these assumptions. Councillor Summerby's indignation at the suggestion that a 'racial incident' might consist of something more insidious and pervasive than the overt forms of racism associated with groups such as the National Front is another common assertion. But others disagree and the lack of agreement over the defining criteria of 'racial' incidents inhibits the development of effective policy responses. Indeed, as we argue in the following chapter, the term 'racial' incidents needs to be deconstructed in order to differentiate between incidents which are legitimated by and expressive of racism and those which involve conflict, in one form or another, between individuals or groups perceived to be racially different. We want to designate the former as racist, the latter as 'racial' or 'inter-racial' incidents.

A third, less obvious, linkage in these articles relates to the salience, or otherwise, of 'race' in the lives of white youngsters living in predominantly white areas of the country. During the course of our research a county adviser for multicultural education informed us that the London *Evening Standard* had summarily dismissed the relevance of Hertfordshire's policy on anti-racism with the phrase: 'Racism in Hertfordshire what next – gay bars in Gateshead!' The proposition that racism is confined to distinctive geographical locales, namely those with a sizeable black (Afro-Caribbean and South Asian origin) population, has a long history, of course. Multicultural education, for instance, was originally conceived as an educational orthodoxy appropriate only as a response to the perceived 'special needs' of black pupils. Despite the intervention of the Swann Committee (DES, 1985) and its insistence that multicultural education should form part of an education for all, irrespective of the location or ethnic mix of schools, this inclusive definition continues to have limited application (Troyna and Carrington, 1990). Yet the evidence of racism in schools where there are only a few black children is unassailable (Akhtar and Stronach, 1986; Gaine, 1987; Mould, 1987). A study commissioned by Lord Swann and his colleagues for their inquiry into the education of ethnic minority children consolidated this evidence. The inquiry concluded that: 'it might generally be felt that racist attitudes and behaviour would be less common in schools with few or no ethnic minority pupils . . . we believe this is regrettably far from the case' (DES, 1985, p. 36).

In 1989 we embarked on a two-year research project (funded by the Economic and Social Research Council) which aimed to clarify the various and interlocking themes encapsulated in these newspaper articles and related pieces. In the preceding ten years or so there had been a discernible shift in the way local education authorities (LEAs) had formulated and implemented policies on multicultural education. An increasing number had 'racialised' their stance to encourage anti-racist initiatives on the agenda of educational reform (Troyna and Williams, 1986). There had also been a trend towards more prescriptive and proscriptive modes of intervention, contrasting with the earlier *laissez-faire* or permissive style which characterised policy initiatives up to the early 1980s.

Another distinguishing feature of recent policy initiatives at LEA (and individual school) level had been advice on how to identify and deal with 'racial' incidents in schools and colleges. In some authorities it was part of an overarching policy to tackle these incidents in all of its services: housing, education, social services and so on. But despite an increased awareness that 'racial' incidents impact on the educational careers, security and welfare of black children, there remains a number of important gaps and limitations in understanding their antecedents, incidence and consequences. In turn, this has inhibited the emergence of an effective policy, not only in response but also in attempts to pre-empt the outbreak of these incidents.

Our research stemmed from the conviction that these incidents could only be understood in relation to the salience of 'race' in children's perceptions and interpretations of their everyday realities. Logically, this could only be addressed by exploring its place in the totality of children's worlds; teasing out, in other words, the ideological lens through which they make sense of that world and act within it. Why, and under what circumstances, does 'race' emerge as an appealing and plausible mode of reasoning for young people? What are the conditions which prompt young children to operationalise 'race' as an organising principle and explanatory framework for their day-to-day judgements and actions? To what extent do racialised understandings of the world suffuse their interaction and relationships with other children? In our efforts to clarify these questions we spent a term in each of three primary schools engaging with pupils aged 10 and 11 in the final two years of their primary education.

As we will see in Chapter 3, much of the research on young children and 'race' has tended to be constructed from quantitative methods. Researchers have been determined to compose a picture of what is happening through the assembling of data which are amenable to statistical analysis. Whilst not entirely disillusioned with the application of this methodology to our field of interest we were clear that its imperatives were incompatible with our own. We were less concerned with documenting and describing the frequency of racist incidents in schools than with digging beneath this ground and uncovering the nutrients on which they feed. We therefore rejected quantitative methods in favour of a qualitative research methodology, broadly defined as ethnography. As Martin Hammersley and Paul Atkinson acknowledge, ethnography embraces an eclectic range of sources of information. Thus,

> The ethnographer participates, overtly or covertly, in people's daily lives for an extended period of time, watching what happens, listening to what is said, asking questions; in fact collecting whatever data are available to throw light on the issues with which he or she is concerned.
>
> (Hammersley and Atkinson, 1989, p. 3)

Whatever specific research approaches might be employed by ethnographers, researchers working within this paradigm are committed, above all else, to exploring 'the routine ways in which people make sense of their world in everyday life' (Hammersley and Atkinson, 1989, p. 3).

The research was based in two neighbouring LEAs in England which to preserve anonymity we'll call 'Greenshire' and 'Woodshire'. Both are Shire counties and black citizens in each of the counties comprise less that 3 per cent of the respective total populations. In Greenshire these communities include citizens of Afro-Caribbean and South Asian origin and are concentrated in the county town. The population of South Asian origin includes mainly Sikhs and Muslims. In Woodshire the black presence is dispersed throughout the county's three main centres. It is represented primarily by citizens of South Asian origin; again, Sikhs and Muslims figure most prominently within these communities.

Both LEAs have produced policy statements on racial equality and these have been augmented by the appointment of advisory and support staff. The adviser in Woodshire informed us that the policy was embedded in 'multiculturalism rather than anti-racism'. He continued: 'We have deliberately not taken a hard confrontational approach with staff because the experience of some of us is that this is often counter-productive.' He conceded that this *laissez-faire* approach often failed to ensure the support of and commitment to multicultural education from local schools. 'There is an official policy', he told us, 'but how far that actually goes through the system is very much another matter'. The policy on racial equality in Greenshire assumed a much higher profile and was propelled by a more vigorous, interventionist procedure. It had also produced guidelines on 'racial' incidents. The adviser in Woodshire recalled how he had tried to develop a policy on 'racial' harassment along the lines recommended by the Home Office in 1989; namely, an overarching policy supported and regulated by all of Woodshire's departments. 'When that came out', he told us, 'I went to see the Deputy County Clerk who didn't want to know and said: "We don't have that problem here, there aren't any racial riots here. We don't need to do anything about it." '

Two of the sample schools were based in Woodshire, the other in Greenshire. Woodshire Primary School is in one of the LEA's main population centres and draws on a catchment area comprising a predominantly working-class community. The headteacher told us that of the 414 pupils on roll there were 'very few children whose parents are from professional classes, or occupations' whilst there was 'a fairly high number of children whose parents don't have jobs'. And the ethnic mix of the school?

In terms of percentage we have approximately 14% of children from ethnic minorities. Of those the majority are of Asian background and the majority of these are Sikh in background.

And we have a handful of children who are Muslim, a couple of Hindus and the rest are Afro-Caribbean.

The staff's perspective on multicultural education corresponded, more or less, with the views espoused in Woodshire's policy document. The headteacher admitted that 'racial' incidents did take place in the school mainly in the form of name-calling. None the less, he did not 'believe it to be a great problem . . . you get name calling about all sorts of things'.

Hillside Junior School is in another of the LEA's major towns. Of the 175 children in the school about two-thirds came from a working-class background, the remainder from a middle-class one. The black population in the school was around 17 per cent: 'mainly Muslim with some Sikhs and Hindus as well as Euro-Caribbean kids', according to the headteacher. Again, the publication of the LEA's policy on multicultural education had made little difference to the prevailing ethos of the school; 'it's not significant', the headteacher told us, 'I would say that the attitude of most teachers would follow that approach anyway. It only reinforces existing attitudes'. For him racism in the school was not 'a problem' – but 'there are problems'. As he put it later: 'The difficulty is in knowing whether that problem has arisen because of racial reasons or the racism has crept in as a weapon as it were in an argument.' He maintained that he would 'come down like a ton of bricks' if he overheard abuse of any kind and that 'racial abuse is high on the list of no-noes'. However, other than 'social training, discussion of people's rights and values and that usual sort of thing' there were no distinctive strategies for dealing with such incidents.

The third school was based over the county border in Greenshire. 'Mainly served by housing estates' according to the headteacher, the school comprised 223 children. Of these, a relatively high proportion, around 25 per cent, were of South Asian origin, the majority of whom were Sikh. Greenshire Community Primary School used the LEA's policy on racial equality as 'something to fall back on if need be' and staff were committed to mounting a full-frontal attack on racism, when necessary. The headteacher told us of the school's policy on anti-racism which ensured that 'we will act on any racist comment'. And what of the LEA's guidelines on recording 'racial' incidents? The headteacher explained:

We have never done that before so that is something now that we will look into and follow up. I think it is very important as well that the non-teaching staff is involved and obviously need to know what we decide in the school. We will hold a meeting of all our dinner supervisors, caretaker, the cooks and everyone that works in the kitchen so that they are aware of what the procedures are and so that if anything happens at lunch-times they can come straight to me and sort it out that way.

She also intended to 'hold meetings with parents about it' and reckoned that 'through educating our own children in this school about racism this has helped a lot with parents'. The school had also developed guidelines on how its staff 'will support a child's culture, background, religion, mother tongue, and that we will make a stance on racist comments that are heard in school'. Its stance on racism, then, was more overt than those of our other sample schools.

We spent one term in each of the three schools, beginning in the autumn term with Woodshire school. Here we carried out an intensive study of one Year 6 class containing thirty-two children. All the children were white apart from two Asian boys and two Asian girls. We also worked with several children in the parallel Year 6 class, in particular with a group of four girls, two of whom were White, and two Afro-Caribbean. Six months later, at the end of the summer term, we returned to this school for several days.

In Hillside school we worked with one Year 6 class of thirty-one children, with three Asian boys and one Asian girl. We also worked, though less intensively, with a parallel class which contained a mixture of Year 6 and Year 5 children, including three Asian boys, one Asian girl and an Afro-Caribbean boy.

We spent the summer term in Greenshire school, studying two parallel classes of mixed Year 4 and Year 5 children. There was a total of 77 children, of whom 15 were black: 7 Asian girls, 6 Asian boys, and 2 Afro-Caribbean girls.

We explained to the children that our purpose in the school was to gather material for a book about children. We did not specify any particular interest in issues of 'race'. The bulk of our research took the form of discussions with children, individually and in small self-selected groups, outside the classroom situation. These discussions did not follow a previously structured format. There was of course a number of themes that we wanted to explore, revolving mainly around their ideas about issues of 'race' and their experiences of 'race' in their own lives. But we had the time to allow discussions to take their course, to let the children talk about what mattered to them and to pick up and respond to issues that they raised. We didn't talk only about issues of 'race', or necessarily even mainly about it in any particular session. We talked to all the children on several occasions, for periods of time ranging from half an hour to, in the case of one group on one occasion, an entire school day. Sometimes we used materials to stimulate discussion: photographs, some taken by the children, some of other schools, stories, poems and case-studies. But in general the children needed no stimulus apart from the opportunity to talk freely to an adult who wasn't taking the role of a teacher, who promised to treat everything they said in complete confidence, and who was willing to listen sympathetically and take seriously whatever they wanted to say, without making judgements.

In addition to our discussions we used a number of other approaches. We spent break-times and lunch-times with the children, we shadowed some children during their school day, we carried out surveys of relationships among the children, and some of them wrote diaries for us. But the approach that provided by far the richest data was simply talking with the children.

Before turning to our own empirical research we want to spend the next two chapters appraising critically what is currently available in the literature on 'racial' incidents in general, and then focus on how researchers have explored the institutional and social worlds of children from the perspective of 'race' and ethnicity.

Chapter 2

Feeling harassed?
Racist incidents in Britain

The eruption of racist incidents in British schools is not a new phenomenon. Despite the perceptible increase in concern shown by central and local government, teacher unions, the Commission for Racial Equality and its local councils throughout the 1980s, black youngsters have experienced physical and verbal abuse and the deprecation of their ethnic and cultural backgrounds for some considerable time. 'Being racially harassed is a way of life' is how one Community Relations Officer put it to the Swann Committee (DES, 1985, p. 33).

In this chapter we want to do two things. We will begin by outlining the nature and extent of racist incidents in education since the late 1960s and give some flavour of the dominant interpretive frameworks used by educationists and others in framing a response to its incidence. We will then move on to the thorny issue of how best to define the term 'racist incident'. Here we will argue for a firm distinction between racist incidents and the more common descriptions: 'racial incidents' and 'inter-racial conflict'. The rationale for this and the following chapter might be said to stem from Stuart Hall's conviction that the purpose of theorising is to 'enable us to grasp, understand and explain – to produce a more adequate knowledge of the historical world and its processes; and thereby to inform our practice so that we might transform it' (Hall, 1988, p. 36). It will soon become clear that we are entering a field of enquiry which is characterised by a lack of conceptual precision, an absence of theory-based explanations, a predominance of anecdotal and other descriptive material and confusion about what might constitute an effective policy to combat the outbreak of racist incidents. Clearly, if we are to respond constructively to such incidents, deal appropriately with victims and perpetrators and, above all, be more successful in pre-empting racist incidents in classrooms and playgrounds we need to base policies and practices on a fuller and more sophisticated understanding of those factors which precipitate their eruption.

'THE MYTH OF FAIRNESS'

Looking back over the last twenty-five years or so we can periodise those phases when racist incidents in and around the school gates generated a 'moral panic' in Britain. The 'Paki-Bashing' episodes of the 1960s and 1970s; the mobilisation of youth recruitment drives by the National Front (NF) and British Movement (BM) during the mid to late 1970s; and localised racist activities in and around schools in London, Coventry and elsewhere in the early 1980s each threw the political spotlight on this issue, for a short time at least. On the face of it, we might have expected the multicultural education policies emerging from LEAs, teacher unions and individual schools after 1978 to have centralised and responded to these incidents. They did not. Despite the escalation of racist activities around this time and the formation of anti-racist groups in and outside education (ALTARF, 1984; Widgery, 1986; Troyna and Carrington, 1990), education policymakers – including both elected members and professional officers – carefully circumvented the issue of racism and its corrosive impact in education in the framing of their multicultural policies. The resulting documents were 'deracialised': they gave priority to cultural pluralism, not anti-racism – the life styles not life chances of black youngsters.

From the sketchy picture we are able to draw it seems that educationists in Town and County Halls as well as those on the 'chalk face' failed to appreciate that racist harassment, in its broadest sense, constituted a significant issue for schools. A clear example of this myopia can be found in research carried out in the late 1960s, the time of the first wave of 'skinheadism' in Britain. As part of their study of skinhead culture in the East End of London, Sue Daniel and Pete McGuire (1972) contacted local educationists to establish their opinions on this new youth movement. They found that headteachers were stubbornly resistant to the view that the skinhead sub-culture and the racism it celebrated had any relevance to their schools. The headteacher of Robert Montefiore school in Bethnal Green put it like this: 'we never had and we do not presently have any Skinheads or skinhead element in this school' (Daniel and McGuire, 1972, p. 39). But this bore little resemblance to what Daniel and McGuire learned from their contact with the local youths. The skinheads who had attended the school spoke in ways that suggested that the potential for racist harassment was never far below the surface. As one gang member said:

> Me and Bob used to go to school at Robert Montefiore and there used to be Pakis . . . I just about scraped to keep in the 'A' class, whereas Bob was just below me and he kept going down and 'e was in 'B' and 'C' and so 'e knew 'em and they was all Pakis and 'e'd be in school 'ello, so and so, all right? and 'e'd go 'ome at night and beat 'em up, beat their dads up.
>
> (Daniel and McGuire, 1972, p. 39)

The tendency for educationists to export the problem of racism to somewhere, almost anywhere beyond the school gates prevailed throughout the 1970s (Troyna and Williams, 1986). Yet that decade witnessed a growth in the popularity of fascist groups such as the NF and BM which in turn presaged a dramatic rise in the incidence of physical intimidation and verbal abuse of Britain's black citizens and their children (Bethnal Green and Stepney Trades Council, 1978; Widgery, 1986; Cohen and Bains, 1988, for example). Associated with this development were two relatively new and insidious trends. First, in contrast to the racist attacks on black people in Britain in the earlier part of the twentieth century and in Nottingham and Notting Hill in 1958, there was a distinct move from collective to individualised violence (Holmes, 1988; Joshua, *et al.*, 1983). The murder of Gurdip Singh Chaggar outside a public house in Southall, West London in 1976 and the fatal stabbing of Altab Ali in East London two years later exemplified this pattern. Second, perpetrators of this violence tended to depersonalise their victim. 'Doing a Paki' became a resonant theme from the late 1960s onwards. David Widgery recalls how the two teenage assailants on Altab Ali considered their victim a legitimate target 'simply by being an Asian' (Widgery, 1986, p. 16). Sean Carey picked up this theme in his conversations with members of the 'Teviot', a gang based in a council housing estate in the Tower Hamlets area of London. Frank told the researcher: 'I just hate 'em that's all.' He continued: 'Like, if I see a Paki walking round here now and I hadn't gone away, I'd just hammer him' (Carey, 1985, p. 124).

'Doing a Paki', and its translation into a wave of racist incidents in schools, was given further momentum in the mid to late 1970s when fascist organisations in Britain contrived to secure a tighter relationship with white (male) youths, especially in major urban centres. In 1977 the NF established a youth movement, the YNF, and in the following year launched a campaign in which it circulated inflammatory racist literature around schools up and down the country. This was followed by the distribution of *How to Spot a Red Teacher* and *How to Combat a Red Teacher*, publications which encouraged white youngsters to challenge the legitimacy of multi-racial education and other so-called Marxian ideologies. Although Stan Taylor is probably correct in suggesting that the YNF's campaign 'did not amount to a great deal' (Taylor, 1982, p. 142) it certainly gave the clue to what was to become the NF and BM's vigorous assault on youth in the months following the 1979 General Election. The dismal failure of the NF to secure electoral support, alongside the re-organisation of the BM under the leadership of Michael McLaughlin prompted a radical change in the party's strategy. Both eschewed what had been, self-evidently, a superficial veneer of political respectability. In its place they concentrated on developing the policies of intimidation and agitation. In this scenario, their target was white youth; the setting for recruitment and racist activities: football grounds, rock concerts, the streets and schools; their immediate goal: inciting a series of racist incidents in Britain's major urban areas (Murdock and Troyna, 1981).

As we have already seen, the nascent multicultural education policies which coincided with these latest flurries of racist activity had little, if anything, to say about racism. Ostensibly, the National Union of Teachers' booklet, *Combating Racism in Schools* (1981) proved the exception. Or did it? Prompted by a concern with NF and BM incursions into the social and institutional worlds of pupils, and the potential for more widespread racist incidents in schools, the NUT recommended its members to produce institutional policies which would confirm publicly that: 'the school will not tolerate, or condone through inaction, any form of racist behaviour' (National Union of Teachers, 1981, p. 3). This certainly looked like a step in the right direction; a tentative move towards recognising that schools had a part to play in the prevention or containment of racism and the incidents it sparked off. But the document suffered from important substantive and theoretical weaknesses. First of all, its focus was on reaction, not prevention. Its emphasis was proscription: the banning of racist graffiti, insignia, uniform, publications and abuse. Second, it sanctioned what Julian Henriques defines as the 'rotten apple theory' of racism. It encouraged the view that racist incidents were constituted, purely and simply, as an 'individualised, exceptional phenomenon' (Henriques, 1984, p. 62). Something out of the ordinary; the property of an individual (or group) who has deviated from the accepted (and acceptable) norms of the society. As Henriques points out, this portrayal of racism logically exonerates society, as a whole, from responsibility. We can see how the NUT colludes in this understanding by its reference to the way 'ignorant and prejudiced attitudes amongst pupils' might destabilise relationships within schools and how these could be dealt with by 'a curriculum which encourages cultural diversity and which fosters mutual respect between ethnic groups' (National Union of Teachers, 1981, p. 2). This is the multicultural paradigm in its exemplary form, anchored to and legitimated by the 'rotten apple theory' of racism. It conceives of racism as no more or less than individual racial prejudice which in turn stems from ignorance. The solution: a rationalist pedagogy and a curriculum suffused by cultural pluralism to dislodge prejudice and educate 'the ignorant'. Accordingly racism is neither institutionalised nor normative in British society: it's an aberration, according to this perspective.

So, despite its ostensibly radical, anti-racist rhetoric, the NUT document reproduced a multicultural paradigm; a perspective, that is, which helped to sustain what Colin Holmes (1985) calls 'the myth of fairness' in British society. During the 1980s when politicians and governmental departments and agencies began to show increasing awareness and anxiety over the profusion of racist incidents in schools (and beyond), this myth and the status of tolerance 'in the pantheon of national values' (Samuel, 1989, p. xvi) remained unassailable. We can see it in full flow in Sir Keith Joseph's (1985) valedictory speech as Secretary of State for Education and Science where he discussed education for an ethnically mixed society. Whilst he did not 'deny that in our society, just as in other societies, there is prejudice against ethnic minorities' this was, in his view, 'accompanied by ignorance' and could be contrasted with 'the tradition of tolerance which is one of British society's most precious values'. Against this background Joseph insisted that calls for wide-ranging multicultural and, especially anti-racist, education programmes were spurious.

But it was a view which chimed discordantly with emerging evidence about racism in schools. In the same year as Joseph's speech, Lord Swann and his colleagues asserted that it was 'difficult for ethnic minority communities to have full confidence and trust in an institution which they see as simply ignoring or discussing what is in fact an ever present and all pervasive shadow over their everyday lives' (DES, 1985, p. 35). This concern with the prevalence of racist incidents was not confined to urban schools. Indeed, as we saw in the previous chapter Swann contended that the impact was 'particularly strong when [black pupils] are present in relatively small numbers in schools and are thus less able to be mutually supportive in the face of racial abuse' (DES, 1985, p. 33). The evidence submitted by the Department of Education and Science (DES) to the Home Affairs Committee report on the Bangladeshi community in 1986; the Commission for Racial Equality's (CRE) series of case studies on racist incidents in *Learning in Terror* (CRE, 1987b) and material collected by journalists, local monitoring groups, researchers and the Home Affairs Committee in 1989 corroborated the views of the Swann Committee. Racist incidents were neither rare nor geographically contained. On the contrary, they were common and widely dispersed, a pervasive, even day-to-day experience of many pupils of Afro-Caribbean and South Asian origin. In the words of the Home Affairs Committee, racist harassment is one of the most 'frightening realities' for black citizens and their children (Home Affairs Committee, 1989, p. xiv).

As the 1980s were drawing to a close it was becoming evident that racist harassment, though often equated purely and simply with overt physical attacks on black people and their property, comprised a broader range of less easily detectable, more subtle and therefore more common set of experiences. This was acknowledged by the Home Office in its report *The Response to Racial Attacks and Harassment* (1989). Published in association with the DES and other government agencies, it insisted that apparently 'trivial incidents' such as 'jostling in the street, racial abuse by children and teenagers, insulting behaviour by neighbours' and so on cumulatively created 'an insidious atmosphere of racial harassment and intimidation' (Home Office, 1989, para 11). Rather ominously, perhaps, the recommendations of this inter-departmental report seem to have been ignored.

'ANY DISTINGUISHING MARK'?

The move towards recognising that racist harassment (and cognate terms such as racist incidents, racist attacks, racist bullying and racist abuse) is an inclusive rather than exclusive concept has not been accompanied by greater clarity over the criteria which identify uniquely such occurrences. It remains the case, as Lucy Bonnerjea and Jean Lawton point out, that most writers in this field use 'descriptions rather than definitions' (Bonnerjea and Lawton, 1988, p. 2). This is lamentable and is a stock example of the impoverished theoretical terrain on which most studies in this have been based. Yet, as Bonnerjea and Lawton inform us:

> Definitions are, however, important both for studies which set out specifically to quantify problems, as well as for the general understanding of assumptions, stereotypes and myths which operate about 'inter-racial incidents'.
>
> (Bonnerjea and Lawton, 1988, p. 3)

One of these myths centres on the alleged insignificance of 'race' in many of the incidents.

The 'playing down' of race in such incidents characterised Norman Tebbit's argument in *The Independent Magazine* where he denounced Salman Rushdie as 'an unwelcome, impertinent, whining guest' (8 September 1990). Tebbit referred to Rushdie's recollections of his experiences at Rugby school where he suffered racist abuse from his fellow pupils and castigated Rushdie for allowing these 'taunts' to become the 'chips he has carried through life'. In Tebbit's view the experience should be seen as typical of the routine, often conflictual, interaction between schoolchildren; no more or less significant or hurtful than 'schoolboy taunts at the expense of fat, tall, thin, short, left-handed, red-haired boys' in fact, 'any distinguishing mark' (Tebbit, 1990, p. 54). Tebbit's position, here, is by no means uncommon and we will see in later chapters that it is shared by many parents, teachers and children. However, it is discrepant with the views of the Swann Committee which emphasised the particular salience of 'race' in such contexts. 'Racist name-calling', according to the Committee, can 'convey to a child the accepted value judgement which the majority community has passed on his or her community' (DES, 1985, p. 35). This is interesting. Not only does the Swann Committee confer primacy on 'race' in its interpretation of the motivation behind and experience of this form of abuse, it goes beyond the definitions (and explanations) offered by the CRE (1987a) and Home Affairs Committee (1989) in differentiating between *racist* incidents and the genre of *racial* incidents and inter-*racial* conflict. It's a distinction which we want to maintain here. For the CRE, inter-racial conflict represents various 'kinds of anti-social behaviour [which] may be experienced by everyone regardless of race' (CRE, 1987a, p. 7). Similarly, the Home Affairs Committee accepted the definition of a 'racial' incident which had been proposed by the Association of Chief Police Officers (ACPO) in England, Wales and Northern Ireland. Namely:

> any incident in which it appears to the reporting or investigating officers that the complaint involves an element of racial motivation; or any incident which includes an allegation of racial motivation made by any person.
>
> (Home Affairs Committee, 1989, p. v)

It seems to us that these are not stipulative definitions and therefore lack explanatory power. Simply put, they do not provide the analytical tools for clarifying and interpreting the incidence of conflict between black and white youngsters and adults. For instance, how do they help us to account for the two dominant patterns presented in the available research: that black people are more liable to experience 'racially' motivated harassment (in all its forms) than their white counterparts (Home Office, 1981); and that black children are most frequently picked out for 'racial' abuse by their white peers in school (Kelly, 1990). Quite obviously these operational definitions do not help us explain these patterns: they obscure rather than clarify the nature of these trends. This is because they fail to acknowledge the asymmetrical power relations between black and white citizens in Britain and are insensitive to the extent to which the harassment and abuse of Blacks by Whites is expressive of the ideology which underpins that relationship: racism. At its basic common denominator, then, a racist incident is about the misuse of power: the collective power enjoyed by White people in a society characterised by racist ideologies and discriminatory practices. It is on these grounds that we reject the all-embracing nomenclatures of 'racial incidents' and 'inter-racial conflict' which the CRE, Home Office and others endorse. We are committed to ensuring a clear distinction between attacks of whatever form, by Whites on Blacks and those perpetrated by Blacks on white people. So, it is not simply a matter of semantics. The distinction goes straight to the heart of our theoretical positioning of this phenomenon and the way we seek to interpret and deal with its occurrence. Along with Paul Gordon we are convinced that, it is only by recognising the nature of racially-motivated attacks on Black people that one can begin to tackle the problem. To confuse such attacks with ordinary criminal attacks, or to claim, in the absence of any such evidence, that attacks by Black people on White people are 'racial' is to render the concept of racism quite meaningless.

(Gordon, 1986, p. 5)

Chapter 3

Friend or foe?
Relationships between black and white children in school

'VERY LITTLE KNOWLEDGE'

'It is difficult to get a reliable picture of the state of race relations in schools' claimed Her Majesty's Inspectorate (HMI) in 1984. Nor can we dissent from this conclusion. Yet, it is both remarkable and regrettable, contrasting, for instance, with a considerable growth in interest in within-school processes and particularly social relationships between pupils, and with their teachers. Certainly, it can no longer be confidently asserted, that 'studies of pupils' experience of schools' are "a novelty" (Hammersley and Woods, 1984, p. 1). Yet with one or two recent exceptions (Gillborn, 1990, Mac an Ghaill, 1988), relationships between black and white children, especially in primary schools, have been conspicuously absent from empirical studies. Andrew Pollard's influential study, *The Social World of the Primary School* (1985), exemplifies this point. The thrust of the book is an analysis of children's perspectives during their final year of an 8–12 middle school. Whilst he based the research in a multi-ethnic school, Pollard did not include the black children in his published study and construction of analytical 'types' of friendship groups. This 'invisibility' is also at odds with the emerging literature on the nature of relationships between older youths in multi-ethnic neighbourhoods and youth clubs (Back, 1991; Hewitt, 1986; Jones, 1988; Walker, 1988). In these studies researchers have eschewed quantitative methods in favour of more penetrative, ethnographic approaches to the analysis of friendship patterns within and across ethnic (and gender) lines. This has provided a more sensitive understanding of how issues of ethnicity and 'race' figure as part of the totality of the social and institutional worlds of these youths.

Michael Marland is only exaggerating slightly, then, when he asserts that: 'there is very little knowledge, except the picturesquely anecdotal, of the detailed texture of school life from the point of view of ethnicity' (Marland, 1987, p. 119). In broad terms, it's possible to identify three discernible and enduring strands of interest in this area of inquiry. First, a long-standing concern to establish the attitudes of young children towards their own and other ethnic groups. We will argue that these studies are commonly enacted under experimental conditions and are based largely on the conviction that the results have certain predictive properties. That is, to represent and anticipate general patterns of interaction between black and white youngsters, in and outside school. The second area of interest has been with actual patterns of interaction between children and their relationship to ethnicity. Here, a quantitative research method known as sociometry has been applied to try to establish how far ethnicity informs the formation and structure of school-based friendship groupings. Finally, researchers in recent years have shown an interest in 'racial' incidents, especially those involving physical and verbal abuse. In our view these studies have only scratched the surface of this complex and volatile issue. The discursive, often anecdotal portraits of 'racial' harassment on the one hand, are augmented by what we see as limited (and limiting) quantitative assessments of the incidence of 'racial' incidents on the other, to reveal – if that's the appropriate word – a superficial, often contradictory set of data.

As a backcloth to our own research material we need to spend some time looking critically at the way these studies have been conceptualised and implemented. Without wishing to pre-empt our appraisal we believe that the paucity of these studies confirm HMI's claim that 'little is actually known about race relations in schools' (Her Majesty's Inspectorate, 1984, p. 1). We will then go on to sketch out the theoretical influences which have guided our own research inquiries and which, we believe, provide us with a greater insight into this area.

CHILDREN'S RACIALISED ATTITUDES

The determination to tease out black children's group and self-image through various experimental research techniques stretches back to the late 1930s and the pioneering work of Kenneth and Mamie Clark (1939) in the USA. Using photographs of members of different ethnic groups and, in the Clarks' later study (1947), different coloured dolls, black children were asked to select the appropriate representation in response to a range of questions associated with their ethnicity: how they identified themselves; their preferred identity; and their perception of ethnic differences. The research uncovered a strong trend towards apparent misidentification amongst black children. They were shown to express a preference for being white; findings which had important and durable effects on the framing of educational policy. It was inferred from these identity studies that black children had negative group- and self-images, had internalised and given credence to the low status accorded their culture by the dominant ethnic group- and that, consequentially, this undermined their feelings of self-worth, motivation to succeed and, as a corollary, inhibited their educational potential. In this scenario, schools were exhorted to take ameliorative action. How? By providing positive reinforcement of the expressive and historical features of black culture. The identity studies of the immediate post-war years sounded the death-knell for monocultural forms of education in the USA. Out of its ashes rose, first, the intercultural, then multicultural education movement (Olneck, 1990).

Concern with the attitudes of white children towards other ethnic groups has an even longer history. In 1929 Bruno Lasker used a postal questionnaire to elicit adults' views of children's 'racial' attitudes. Despite the crude and questionable status of his research methods Lasker's conclusions were remarkably prescient in acknowledging how young children are 'made to notice outer differences and to accept them as signs of inner differences of value' (Lasker, 1929, p. 370). Both in the USA and Britain research findings derived from these and other theoretical and methodological positions have confirmed and extended Lasker's initial diagnosis (see Aboud, 1988; Carrington and Short, 1989 for reviews of the literature).

In Britain, identity studies informed by similar social psychological perspectives have established an equally firm footing in the literature on race relations in education and in the development of educational policies and associated practices. The educational, if not political, rationale for nascent multicultural education initiatives at the cusp of the 1970s and 1980s derived at least in part from the influential research of David Milner (1975; 1983) and later, Alfred Davey (1983). Following the conceptual, methodological and interpretive path laid down by the Clarks in the USA, Milner and Davey cited the results of their respective identity studies to challenge the efficacy of monocultural education and the assimilationist ideology on which it was based. They recognised that the degree of alleged misidentification and 'out-group preferment' (as it's called) of black children had diminished with the passage of time, partly because of the rise in black nationalism in the 1960s and 1970s. None the less, they insisted that their research revealed clear evidence of the maintenance of this trend.

We say 'alleged' misidentification and 'out-group preferment' because this research orthodoxy has been subjected to serious criticism, especially by black social scientists such as Maureen Stone (1981) and Olivia Foster-Carter (1986). It's not necessary to rehearse all their objections here. But we do need to ask what contribution these studies have made to our understanding of race relations between children in schools. In the light of the criticisms made by Stone, Foster-Carter and others it's tempting to reply: 'not very much'. But this would be oversimplifying the issue. As Davey pointed out in his response to Foster-Carter's summary dismissal of this research tradition: 'There is no doubt that some investigators went beyond the evidence of their data in intuiting personal qualities which could have been better ascertained by more direct methods.' However, in his view there was still insufficient grounds for the 'proposed invalidation of some 40 years of research' (Davey, 1987, p. 481). We agree. The identity studies and complementary research on white children's attitudes towards other ethnic groups have demonstrated beyond any doubt that young people are 'racialised' by the time they experience primary school education. We recognise that this goes against the grain of common-sense assumptions about childhood innocence which constitute one of the main tenets of the ideology of primary education (Alexander, 1984). This conception of childhood is fairly widespread, as we saw in the opening chapter and has helped to discourage a number of primary school teachers from involving their pupils in discussions about race-related and other controversial issues (see Carrington and Troyna, 1988 for discussion). None the less, as the research following Lasker's study continues to show, it's both an idealised and false image of the way young children perceive and interpret their social worlds. But what of the weaknesses of the 'racial attitude' studies?

Putting to one side momentarily our concern about the way researchers have interpreted the apparent predilection of black children to reject 'same-race' dolls and photographs in favour of representatives of the dominant ethnic group, it's our conviction that these studies suffer from delusions of grandeur. Implicitly or otherwise, researchers working in this theoretical mode have encouraged a belief in the predictive powers of these studies. In other words, they presume that the nature of race relations in schools and elsewhere can be 'read off' from the findings. This sits uneasily alongside the now well established fact that there is only a tenuous relationship between attitudes (especially those expressed under experimental conditions) and actual behaviour. As Gordon Allport put it almost forty years ago, children might articulate and reproduce a racist discourse but this need not necessarily operate as an informing principle of their day-to-day interaction. His controversial view was that children's rejection of other ethnic groups is 'chiefly verbal'. Thus, 'While they may damn the Jews, the wops, the Catholics, they may still *behave* in a relatively democratic manner' (Allport, 1954, p. 310; original emphasis). The truth or falsity of Allport's claim requires further systematic and empirical scrutiny, of course. The point we wish to make is that there is no necessary or automatic link between attitudes and actions and we must therefore be cautious in responding to these studies.

'Quantitative methods' according to Liz Gordon, 'can only report what is happening; qualitative look at the why and the how' (Gordon, 1984, p. 106). In both the identity studies and the more general investigation of children's 'racial' attitudes researchers have given priority to the 'what'. Their principal concern has been with eliciting and documenting the nature of children's perceptions and conceptions of race-related issues rather than exploring the processes which underpin those attitudes. Consequently, the stimuli presented to these children (dolls, photographs, word association tests, sentence completion tasks and so on) and the way questions are framed ('Give me the doll (or photograph) that looks like a white child?' The English are . . .?') give excessive weight to physical features. Although decontextualised and disembodied these physical traits are presented to children as legitimate criteria for differentiating humankind – and the children, for obvious reasons to do with the power relations between researcher and 'researched' – are constrained to respond in similar terms. Quite apart from the dubious ethical and political premises of this strategy (see Troyna and Carrington, 1989) it seems almost inevitable that 'racial' and 'ethnic' characteristics will be used by children in their responses; after all, it's the only resource available to them! It seems difficult to argue with the view that the research is manipulated to ensure that children's perceptions and responses are 'colour-struck', to use Foster-Carter's term (1986).

These caveats do not lead us to believe that theories about children's 'racial' attitudes are simply an artefact of this methodology. As we have already noted, supportive evidence for young children's 'racialised' perceptions of social reality are available from other sources (Carrington and Short, 1989; Menter, 1989). But we are convinced that researchers working within this paradigm have tended to sacrifice understandings of the process of racialisation on the altar of description. Stephen Reicher argues along similar lines in his critique of Davey's work. He maintains that the use of still photographs in the study naturalises 'race' and sex which are:

> the archetypes for justifying the physical categorisation of humanity. Such a method ignores that many alternative forms of categorisation, for instance class, depend on what people do rather than, principally, how they look. The only way to guard against such implicit bias is to start off by examining the ordinary language explanations of 'naturally' occurring events ... Instead of simply applying quantitative techniques to limited response categories, it is necessary to use qualitative analyses in order to establish the categorical structure prior to statistical analysis.
>
> (Reicher, 1986, p. 165)

This seems to us to be one of the main purposes of social science; to 'deconstruct the obvious' (Hall, 1980, p. 6), not encourage, reproduce and legitimate what are in this instance invidious and divisive, even racist forms of categorisation.

FRIEND OR FOE?

The second main strand of our 'knowledge' of race relations between pupils derives from a concern to identify and explain the salience, or otherwise, of ethnicity in the structure of school-based friendship groups. Again, quantitative methods, with few noticeable exceptions (Denscombe, *et al.*, 1986; Grugeon and Woods, 1990) have been used to explore this pattern. The favoured approach is sociometry. Here, children are asked to nominate their three best friends in school, who they would like to sit or play with, or some such variant. The results are then presented either in tabular or diagrammatic form. This shows the cluster of friendships both in numerical terms (the size and range of groups) and how they are constituted in relation to ethnicity (and other structural or organisational variables). Summing up the research findings on ethnicity and friendship groups in schools in

Britain, Sally Tomlinson writes that pupils 'do not appear to form inter-ethnic friendships to any great extent, being "racially aware" and preferring their own groups from an early age' (Tomlinson, 1983, p. 129). If this is true then it is especially worrying for those who subscribe to the 'contact hypothesis'. This is the conviction that interpersonal contact across ethnic lines, in and of itself, brings about better race relations by attenuating individual racial prejudice. If segregated groups continue to prevail in multi-ethnic schools, as Tomlinson's distillation of sociometric research findings suggests, then there seems little hope of improved race relations in the future, according to this theory of intergroup behaviour.

However, if the study of friendship groups in multi-ethnic classrooms and schools is to contribute substantively to our understanding of pupil relationships in those settings, we need to consider two things. First, whether it is reasonable to infer from quantitative research that ethnicity is a salient, perhaps determining feature of friendship formations. This is certainly what sociometrists allege; but can it be verified? Second, does the structure of these groups have the predictive or generalisable properties which researchers lead us to believe?

In interpreting the rationale underpinning the structure of friendship groups in multi-ethnic settings sociometrists constantly place 'race' or ethnicity in the driving seat. Their results are presented and analysed primarily in relation to these variables (Jelinek and Brittan, 1975; Kawwa, 1968; Kitwood and Borrill, 1980). In so doing, interpersonal behaviour is explained in terms of group characteristics. Put another way the children's motivation for selecting friends is seen in relation to group categories not personal attributes. This seems a dubious, if not entirely invalid interpretation. None the less, it is a common theme running through sociometric analysis. We will hold our criticisms of this interpretation in abeyance briefly whilst we look at other approaches to studies of friendship groups in multi-ethnic schools.

During the course of some research into development education in primary schools, Martyn Denscombe and his colleagues (1986) found that the apparent tendency for 'in-group' choices revealed through sociometric tests dissented from teachers' perceptions of the ethnic composition of their pupils' friendship groups. According to the teachers the make-up of these groups routinely transcended ethnic boundaries. In an attempt to explain this contradiction, Denscombe and his research workers complemented their sociometric analysis of friendship groups in a multi-ethnic junior school with more qualitative, observational research methods. They concluded that sociometry was too abstract and projective to capture the subtle nuances and dynamics of pupil interaction. They found, for instance, that the processes of interaction varied in a range of settings within the school. One of their case study pupils was Sukbhir Singh an 8-year-old Sikh boy. In the sociometric test he had made three 'in-group' choices, that is, Sikh children. But when the research team observed Sukbhir during free association in class and playground activities they found that there was little sign of ethnic exclusivity in his interaction with other pupils. Denscombe and his team acknowledged that neither sociometry nor field observation can tap 'the meaning of friendship for those involved'. However, ethnographic approaches reveal that 'exclusive reliance' on quantitative methods, especially sociometry, cannot hope to explore meaningfully the complexities and dynamism of pupil friendship patterns (Denscombe et al., 1986, p. 233). All they provide is a snapshot picture.

The cleavage between pupils from different ethnic backgrounds might be more apparent than real; an artefact of sociometry which, by its very nature, constrains, rigidifies and over-exaggerates the significance of pupils' friendship nominations. Indeed, circumstantial support for this can be found not only in the qualitative research of Denscombe and his colleagues and in Elizabeth Grugeon and Peter Woods's study in another multi-ethnic primary school (1990) but also in other quantitative methods which, unlike sociometry, do not impose such limits on children's choices (Thomas, 1984). Sociometry, then, might lead us to draw an unduly negative picture of inter-ethnic relationships amongst children, a tendency which is exacerbated by the restrictive interpretive framework in which sociometric data are located and analysed. In a context in which the significance of 'race' and ethnicity is heavily emphasised by researchers in the conception of their studies it is hardly surprising that these variables take centre stage in subsequent attempts to explain social phenomena such as friendship groupings.

Our second question relates to the significance of ethnic preferences in friendships for the broader issue of race relations: the extent to which the pattern of friendship clusters underscores the efficacy of the so-called contact hypothesis. Conventional wisdom does, of course, lead us to believe that inter-ethnic friendships are not only accompanied by, but are signifiers of, the absence of racial prejudice.

Again, this seems an appealing proposition. But it must be treated with some caution.

To begin with the assumption is based on correlational not causal relationships. There might be an observable and statistical link between inter-ethnic friendships and positive racial attitudes of participants but it would be presumptuous to assume that one has a causal relationship to the other. Indeed, even if we could infer causality from this relationship it would be difficult to establish its direction. To paraphrase Reicher: does pupils' involvement in ethnically mixed friendships attenuate their racial prejudice or is it only those (white) pupils who are not racially prejudiced who acquaint themselves with children from other ethnic backgrounds (Reicher, 1986, p. 161). Quantitative research and its commitment to describing rather than explaining what is happening is ill-equipped to answer such a complex question. Furthermore, we cannot presume that pupils' immersion in inter-ethnic friendships is indicative of positive racial attitudes amongst their members. Why? Because this conflates interpersonal relationships with an individual's perception and valuation of groups. This is a crucial distinction. As John Turner (1987) points out in his critique of the contact hypothesis, it is important to differentiate between interpersonal attraction, by which he means favourable attitudes towards people as unique individuals, and group cohesion, the mutual attraction between in-group members *qua* group members. In applying their results to broader discussions about the state of race relations, sociometrists have failed to acknowledge that the relative importance of interpersonal attraction and intergroup relations may vary from one situation to another according to the salience of group membership to individuals in different contexts. In simple terms, then, ethnic homogeneity in school-based friendship groups cannot be assumed automatically to signify negative racial attitudes, or inter-ethnic hostility. Ethnicity may or may not be a significant variable to individuals in that particular setting.

Ethnographic studies of young people's everyday lives have revealed the complex, problematic nature of this issue. For instance, in their exploration of how young white people in the North East of England viewed themselves and their social world, Frank Coffield and his associates uncovered what Raymond Cochrane and Michael Billig (1984) have termed 'the Leroy syndrome' of liking an individual but hating the race she or he comes from' (Coffield *et al.*, 1986, p. 197). In his study of adolescent male youth cultures in Australia, Jim Walker observed a clear example of 'the Leroy syndrome' in an argument over nationality between the 'Aussies' and the Greeks. One of the 'Aussies' insisted that: 'we just wanna beat the Greeks'. The argument continued:

Kazzo: Well fuckin' bash 'im.

Fergo: We do (all talking at once).

Philip: We've been together at this school for ten years and they go (obscene gesture).

Reevsy: We don't, we don't – *we still y'mates, even though y' nothing better than . . .*

Fred: *You're just greasy wogs.*

(Walker, 1988, p. 86; emphasis added)

In everyday discourse this apparent contradiction is often expressed in the phrase, 'Some of my best friends are . . .'. Perhaps the most vivid example of how tension, even discontinuity underlines people's views of individuals on the one hand and their ethnic groups on the other, can be found in Michael Billig's study of prejudice and tolerance as an 'ideological dilemma' (Billig, 1988a). He tells of his encounter with Wendy, a 15-year-old girl in the West Midlands. Immediately after the interview,

conducted at school, this young supporter of a racist party and of compelling all of 'them' to 'leave our country', was to be seen walking arm in arm with a young Asian girl, chatting and laughing in easy friendship.

(Billig, 1988a, p. 106)

We have seen, then, that research on inter-ethnic friendships in school has failed to resolve a number of important questions. It has also made a number of inferential leaps in the interpretation of data. These are at best, dubious, at worst, invalid. Ethnographic studies alongside critical theorisation of the 'contact hypothesis' have gone beyond the snapshot pictures taken by sociometrists to reveal a highly complex, less straightforward interpretation of the nature of friendship groups in ethnically mixed settings. Above all else, they have made painfully clear the limitations of quantitative research in interpreting this aspect of the world of children at school.

RACIST INCIDENTS: 'A WAY OF LIFE'

We have already seen that 'racial' incidents as they are commonly (if often mistakenly) termed have only recently become the focus for systematic research. The 1981 Home Office report on *Racial Attacks*, augmented by the concerns expressed in *Education for All* (DES, 1985) and, of course, the murder of Ahmed Iqbal Ullah at Burnage High School in 1986 (of which we'll have more to say later) have all played a part in securing this issue a place on the research and policy agenda. On the whole, studies have tended to be based in local, rather than national settings: Leeds, Manchester, Birmingham, Glasgow and various parts of inner and outer London. There are exceptions, however. The Commission for Racial Equality (CRE) document, *Learning in Terror* (CRE 1987b) identified 'racial' incidents in and around schools throughout the UK. Similarly, David Smith and Sally Tomlinson's (1989) tentative investigation of 'overt racism' in schools took place in various parts of England.

It is simplifying the picture only slightly to say that the empirical research has been framed around two distinct methodologies. First, local monitoring groups, the CRE, journalists and campaigners, LEAs and specialist enquiry teams have collated an impressive range of evidence to demonstrate the tenacity and pervasiveness of 'racial' incidents in schools. Often this has taken the form of case studies such as those assembled by the CRE (1987b). The second approach has relied on more systematic quantitative methods of analysis. A statistical profile of 'racial' incidents in schools has been built upon pupil responses to questionnaires, word and sentence completion tests, structured classroom observation and interviews with pupils, parents and teachers. Interestingly, and in contrast with the general conclusions drawn from more discursive studies of this issue, quantitative researchers have been more circumspect about the prevalence of 'racial' incidents in schools. Consider, for instance, Elinor Kelly's analysis of 'racial' name-calling in Manchester secondary schools. On the basis of questionnaires completed by 902 pupils she concluded that: 'In thinking about the individuals who may become either "victims" or "aggressors" we are, it seems, talking about a small minority' (Kelly, 1988, p. 27). We will return to Kelly's research later in this chapter. Meanwhile, we can see that Smith and Tomlinson in *The School Effect* (1989) are even less impressed by claims that 'racial' incidents figure prominently on the educational landscape. In their study, parents of children in twenty multi-racial comprehensive schools were asked, amongst other things, about their views on race relations in schools. 'Just 1 per cent of parents mentioned racial attacks, or that black and white children don't get on', according to the researchers (Smith and Tomlinson 1989, p. 62). They contrast their findings with those derived from anecdotal sources and insist that although,

the present study did not include systematic classroom observation, there was little indication of overt racism in relations among pupils or between pupils and staff.

Thus, although some well-publicised reports have created the impression that overt racism is a serious problem in multi-ethnic schools, or in some of them, on closer examination there is little evidence on this matter, and no evidence at all of the size or extent of any problem.

(Smith and Tomlinson, 1989, p. 62)

Nor have their conclusions gone unnoticed by those who have argued vociferously that the issue of racism in schools has been inflated by those with vested interests. This is how Anthony Flew, writing in *Ethnic Enterprise*, responded to Smith and Tomlinson's findings:

The School Effect should remind us all of Hastie's Law: 'The incidence of alleged racism in a given society will vary in direct proportion to the number of people generously paid and prominently positioned to find it.' Never ask the barber whether you need a haircut.

(Flew 1989, p. 2)

So how do we account for the discrepancies between the conclusions drawn from the anecdotal and quantitative measurements of 'racial' incidents? We want to begin by engaging with Smith and Tomlinson's study, partly because of the way it has been enthusiastically received by the media, academics and 'anti-antiracists', partly also because it encapsulates what we see as some of the important weaknesses of existing research into this subject.

It is undoubtedly the case, as Smith and Tomlinson argue, that anecdotal (and, for that matter, much of the supposedly more systematic) empirical evidence on 'racial' incidents is both partial and imprecise. For instance, it fails to provide any indication of how common such incidents might be in schools. Against this, however, we are not convinced that Smith and Tomlinson's study provides a more accurate or sensitive insight. Our reservations crystallise around three concerns.

As they state, their interest is with 'overt racism', by which we take them to mean observable, clear-cut instances of racist abuse, harassment and bullying either by teachers or pupils. As we have already emphasised this is a limited, and simplistic understanding. Previously, we saw that more inclusive definitions have been formulated by the Home Office in association with other central government agencies, LEAs and individual schools in a variety of different situations. These include not only physical and verbal manifestations of racist incidents but also what the London Borough of Waltham Forest describes as 'hidden or indirect forms'. Gloucestershire County Council's document, *Combating Racial Harassment in Schools and Colleges: Guidelines for Positive Action* provides substantive examples of this more broadly conceived interpretation; it includes:

a Physical assault against a person or group because of colour and/or ethnicity.
b Derogatory name-calling, insults, mimicry, racist jokes.
c Racist graffiti.
d Provocative behaviour such as wearing racist badges or insignia.
e Bringing racist materials, such as leaflets, comics, magazines into the school or college.
f Verbal abuse and threats.
g Incitement of others to behave in a racist way.
h Racist comments in the course of any discussion in school or college.
i Attempts to recruit other pupils and students to racist organisations and groups.
j Ridicule of an individual for cultural differences, e.g. food, music, dance, etc.
k Denial of an individual's cultural differences and needs.
l Refusal to co-operate with other people because of their colour and/or ethnic origin.

(Gloucestershire County Council, 1990, p. 4)

The apparent absence of 'overt racism' should not then be used to counter claims about the seriousness or prevalence of racist incidents. The two phenomena are not synonymous. Rather, the former is only one and possibly not the most common expression of the latter.

Smith and Tomlinson's procedure for establishing the incidence of 'overt racism' in their sample schools also gives cause for concern.

The respondents in this part of the study were parents not the pupils. But can parental views be legitimately accepted as providing an accurate and reliable portrayal of racism in schools? It seems not. First, as Smith and Tomlinson imply elsewhere in the study there is a tenuous relationship between what pupils experience at school and parental perceptions of those experiences. The researchers found a weak correlation between 'the child's enthusiasm [for school] as shown by this measure [i.e. questionnaire] and the parents' assessment of how happy the child is at school' (Smith and Tomlinson, 1989, p. 106). This suggests that even if children discuss their schooling experience with their parents they present them with a limited picture: a poorly drawn sketch of their everyday reality of school. It is reasonable to assume that either pupils bracket out their experiences of racism at school from their conversation with parents or, alternatively, that parents reinterpret these experiences. Confirmatory evidence from this can be found in other research. The Macdonald inquiry, for example, noted that Ahmed's sister, Selina Ullah, 'remembered that he would be very reticent about incidents which happened at school and that the family would have to press him *very strongly* in order for him to give any details about incidents which had occurred' (Macdonald *et al.*, 1989, p. 12; emphasis added). Elaine Sihera recalls a similar scenario. Her daughter had been subjected to racist name-calling in her school for some time before she shared the experience with the family. The reason: 'She had not told us because we wouldn't have done much about it' (Sihera, 1988, p. 29). Sihera does not elaborate on the reasons why she would have been reluctant to intervene but Shahnaz Akhtar and Ian Stronach conclude that some parents might trivialise the significance of 'racial' incidents, especially racist name-calling, preferring like Norman Tebbit and others to see it as no better or worse than other forms of teasing and sarcasm between children at school. A Sri-Lankan born mother told Akhtar:

> Normally my children have no problem in school or playground, but sometimes some children call them names such as 'blacky', but I think these are just names during fighting. My children also say to them 'you go sunbathing to make your colour dark'. When I was young in Sri Lanka, children used to call me names such as shorter, Langra (one leg etc.).

> (Akhtar and Stronach, 1986, p. 23)

It could also be that parents trivialise racist name-calling because they feel powerless to intervene in the light of the school's *laissez-faire* perspective on this issue. Whatever the case, it seems that parents can only provide a rough and ready guide to the pervasiveness and expression of racism in their children's everyday experiences at school. It is certainly insufficient ground on which to base a rejection of other, arguably more persuasive, research on this issue.

Our final criticism of Smith and Tomlinson's position centres less on their strategy for establishing the incidence of 'overt racism' in schools, and more on their analytical framework. Once again, we are concerned with the application of quantitative research which we believe is unable to capture the subtle and complex nature of racist incidents. Of course, our critique is not confined to the methodology used in *The School Effect*. It extends to the research of Elinor Kelly (1988), Tessa Cohn (1988) and various projects carried out by local monitoring agencies. Each has concentrated on assembling statistical data on the observable, detectable and therefore easily measurable forms of racism. We have seen that Smith and Tomlinson equate 'racist' incidents with 'overt racism'; Kelly and Cohn meanwhile limit their investigation to physical and verbal abuse.

It seems to us that this determination to use statistical tools of analysis is useful in helping to mobilise action against racist attacks but might also play a part in perpetuating and legitimating reductionist interpretations of these incidents. Perhaps we can express this argument more clearly by looking at parallel tendencies in the cognate field of sexist harassment.

In her critical appraisal of studies of woman battering, Mildred Pagelow (1979) claims that the reliance on statistical methods of investigation has led to superficial and impoverished understanding of this protracted and diffuse phenomenon. The emphasis on statistical profiles means that variables are only conceptualised according to what is easily questionable rather than what is theoretically significant. Thus 'woman battering' is typically defined in research only in terms of physical violence against women. But as Pagelow points out, this excludes verbal and psychological forms of 'woman-battering', forms which are less amenable to quantitative analysis. She continues:

> Numerical tabulation of slaps or kicks produces raw material for the computer to feed upon, but we miss out on more than we get . . . what have we really learned about the interactional dynamics before and after those acts, the actual force of those acts, the

damage sustained (or lack of it) and the cognitions attached to the acts by both the actor and the receiver?

(Pagelow, 1979, p. 346)

She contends that this research othodoxy provides 'skewed results' because it offers limited answers to important questions. For Pagelow, a range of methodologies should be applied to this field of enquiry 'to provide depth as well as breadth to our understanding' (Pagelow, 1979, p. 347).

The study of sexual harassment on campus by Billie Wright Dzeich and Linda Weiner (1984) reached similar conclusions. They argued that the self-imposed silence of female students subjected to 'sexual harassment' by male professors derived in part from uncertainty about how to label those experiences. Again, this highlights the need for a common definition and range of methodologies to facilitate empirical exploration of this phenomenon.

We want to conclude this part of the chapter by turning our attention to the research carried out by Elinor Kelly and Tessa Cohn reported in the monograph, *Racism in Schools – New Research Evidence* (1988). We will see that the determination of those researchers to focus on the surface imagery of racist incidents and to collate the data into statistically acceptable forms reinforces the pertinence and veracity of Pagelow's critique.

Kelly investigated pupils' perceptions of 'racial violence', a study commissioned by the Macdonald inquiry into the murder at Burnage High School in 1986. Based in three secondary schools in Manchester the study tapped the views of 902 pupils, black and white, in the first and fourth years. The research took the form of a written questionnaire although pupils were encouraged to engage in discussion with the research team once the questionnaires were completed. Kelly notes that the questions were framed around two main themes: pupils' personal experiences of teasing and bullying in schools (especially name-calling and fighting), and the names they had heard and fights they had witnessed in schools even if they were not directly involved. In Table 3.1 we can see that each pupil was offered the possibility of mentioning up to three names which made them 'angry or miserable'. One thousand six hundred and six out of a possible 2,706 responses were received from the sample. Of these, only 154 centred on 'racial' names. What the research fails to clarify, however, is where those responses came from. Did 154 children each mention a 'racial'

name or did around 50 offer three different 'racial' names. As
we're not told the ethnic origin of the pupils it is impossible to
ascertain whether it is black or white children who feel 'angry
or miserable' when subjected to this form of verbal abuse. It's
therefore difficult to deduce anything meaningful from these data.

Of course, the critical issue is the ethos which allows racist
name-calling to take place, often with impunity. However, Kelly's
quantitative approach does not facilitate analysis of the schools' ethos
(except in a crude, mechanistic way). All it can provide is a statistical
profile of how common 'racial' names were used as terms of abuse and
clues about the perpetrators and their victims. But even here, we can
see that the research leaves a number of unanswered questions.

We are also told that Asian pupils were more likely to be
subjected to name-calling than their counterparts from other ethnic
backgrounds but neither the nature of this abuse nor the reasons for
the pattern are discussed or explained (Kelly, 1988, p. 13).

Table 3.2 shows that of the 1,504 'names' recalled by children
in the three schools 1,083 were racist; that is, 72 per cent. The
prevalence of racist terms in the pupils' repertoire of abusive
names hardly confirms Kelly's assertion that: 'name-calling may
be endemic among pupils, [but] it does not amount to a cacophony'
(Kelly, 1990, p. 90). At the same time, this statistical overview
does not tell us how frequently black children are called racist
names, what proportion of the names that black children are
called is racist, or what proportion of pupils perpetuated racial
verbal abuse.

Table 3.1 Which names make you angry or miserable?

	First year	Fourth year	Total
Physical	117	52	169
Family	66	64	130
Animal	45	13	58
Anal and Sexual	316	124	440
Racial	75	79	154
Miscellaneous	257	397	654
No response	429	654	1,083
Query	12	6	18
Total	1,317	1,389	2,706

Source: Kelly, 1988, p. 16.

Table 3.2 Which are the racial names you have heard most in school?

	First Year	Fourth Year	Total
Paki	172	306	478
Nigger	102	185	287
Black	67	105	172
Chink	24	47	71
White	14	27	41
Yid	8	26	34
Anal & Sexual	129	17	146
Miscellaneous	152	123	275
No response	644	551	1,195
Query	5	2	7
Total	1,317	1,389	2,706

Source: Kelly, 1988, p. 17.

There is one other quantitative survey of name-calling. Tessa Cohn (1988) elicited the views of 569 pupils aged between 10 and 17 in six schools based in an outer London borough. She found that of all the names cited, 'racist' names were the most common and that the proportion of racist name-calling increased with age. Again, however, the research only scratches the surface. It confirms that racist abuse is part of the repertoire of children's discourse but fails to uncover its role in routine social interaction or the conditions in which it is likely to be expressed.

The picture we have of racist harassment in schools, then, is partial and incomplete. On the one hand, quantitative research has failed to provide a reliable assessment of the frequency or distribution of the incidence of racist harassment. Nor does it have much to say about the victims or perpetrators. On the other, the emphasis on quantitative approaches has precluded a sensitive interpretation (and documentation) of the various expression of racist incidents. To restate our position: like any other pattern of behaviour of children and young people these incidents can only really be understood in the contexts of their lives in home, school and community. The orientation of current research, with its obsession for statistical profiles, has led to a dislocation of racist incidents from these settings. In many ways it might be contended that the atheoretical slant of this research reflects and extends the absence of theory, in general, from studies of racist incidents. Those writers who have attempted to explain the outbreak of such incidents have tended to anchor their analyses in restrictive theoretical strait-jackets. The result? We're left with a number of unanswered questions about the origins and pattern of these incidents, as we will now see.

UNANSWERED QUESTIONS

There are important differences in theory-based explanations for the outbreak of racist incidents in both historical and contemporary settings. In many ways, these differences reflect the macro/micro debate: a key issue in sociology. The former privileges the broader socio-political and economic context in accounting for the outbreak of racist violence, both collective and individual. Theorists working from this perspective accord explanatory status primarily to the intensification of struggle over limited economic, cultural and spatial resources between white indigenous communities and those 'intruders' whom they perceive as illegitimate competitors: black 'immigrants' and their children. This is the theory which is often used to explain the collective forms of violence witnessed in the dockland areas of London, Cardiff, Liverpool and South Shields between 1919 and 1948 as well as more recent incidents. Stephen Humphries' (1981) analysis of why fights broke out between blacks and whites in the late nineteenth and early twentieth centuries is written from the macro perspective. Humphries argues that working-class racism was strained to the limits by the perceived 'invasion' of black immigrants into their established 'space'. This was most keenly experienced in the dockland areas where the 'invasion' coincided with prolonged periods of economic decline. The result:

> racist views developed to provide an immediate explanation for the deterioration of the local neighbourhood and there was an increasing tendency, especially among the unskilled and unemployed, to associate the experience of poverty with the severe competition from immigrants for scarce resources such as jobs and housing . . .
>
> (Humphries, 1981, pp. 193–4)

This is a plausible and attractive explanation. At the same time it is deterministic and mechanistic – an 'occupational hazard' for macro theorists. Their arguments are predicated on the view that there is a causal link between the deterioration of national and local economic conditions and the incidence of racist violence. Unfortunately, it's a proposition that does not stand up to close historical scrutiny. As Colin Holmes (1988) points out, the 1920s and 1930s in Britain were characterised by economic instability and recession but were not marked by any significant or prolonged racist disturbances. It seems that this approach is too broad and all-inclusive to provide sharp explanatory power. After all, a theory which 'explains' the outbreak of violence under certain conditions but ignores its absence in other periods characterised by similar complexion is not an explanation at all.

The micro perspective provides a more localised analysis. Here, the explanatory spotlight is thrown on individual and group interaction, group dynamics, sub-cultural configurations, and the ethos and procedures of institutions. The research on bullying (including racist bullying), tends to be grounded in this approach, as can be testified in the work of Valerie Besag (1989), the Elton Report (1989), and Tattum and Lane (1988). Each has been concerned to tease out the 'typical' characteristics of bullies (and victims) and the organisational features of schools which correlate with a high incidence of bullying. But as Andy Hargeaves has observed, researchers working within the micro perspective are like ostriches: they are 'so preoccupied with the fine-grained detail of school and classroom life' that they rarely take 'their heads out of the sand' to see what is happening in the outside world (Hargreaves, 1985, p. 22). In short, they fail to grab a theoretical toe-hold on the relationship between the interacting-dyad level, the school and society. Researchers engaged in studies of bullying, for instance, provide little more that a perfunctory acknowledgement of those factors beyond the school gates which encourage and legitimate acts of physical aggression, especially amongst boys.

During the last twenty years or so our understanding of children's cultures has been greatly advanced by a number of ethnographic studies of life in schools, strongly influenced by the theoretical perspective provided by symbolic interactionism. The strengths of this approach lie in its focus on the individual in the context of the social group, its concern for the meanings that people bring to social interaction, and its conception of the individual as actively constructing social life. These characteristic features of symbolic interactionism offer particular advantages for studies of life in classrooms and playgrounds.

There is, however, a number of disadvantages with this

perspective and three seem to be particularly pertinent to a study of issues of 'race'. The first is that symbolic interactionism has no concepts to deal with society at the macro level. To be more specific, it is not equipped to account sufficiently for ideologies generated by racialised social structures. This weakness of theory at the level of society as a whole makes it difficult for symbolic interactionism to address the relationship between the macro and micro. Typically, the key concepts of symbolic interactionist studies of education, such as 'interests-at-hand' and 'coping strategies', focus on the pragmatics of the immediate interpersonal situation, that is, the micro level. They don't address how social situations themselves are constructed within ideology and social structure.

The absence of a concept of social structure entails the absence of a concept of *conflict* within social structure. The result is a tendency for symbolic interactionists to focus on the social construction of consensus. Conflict is seen as central to life in schools, but the emphasis is on how conflicting interests are pragmatically reconciled into a 'working consensus'. Consequently, the key concepts used by symbolic interactionist studies of schools deal with processes of adaptation and accommodation. This emphasis on adaptation gives symbolic interactionist analyses a functionalist character.

The two features we have noted, the neglect of ideology and the emphasis on consensus, combine to create a third problem, and that is the unitary conception of the self within symbolic interactionism. Conflict is external; individuals deal rationally with it by distancing themselves from the social roles that they play. There is no notion of conflicting ideologies working within the individual to create inconsistent and contradictory forms of understanding and behaviour.

There have, then, been few, if any, successful attempts to broach, never mind breach the gap between macro and micro analysis – particularly in the research on racist incidents – in or out of school. In fact, as Christopher Husbands concludes from his overview of the literature on racist attacks in Britain, 'there remain a whole series of unanswered questions about the precise circumstances attending these events and the detailed reasons for their perpetration' (Husbands, 1989, p. 91). We need to fill this gap with an overarching framework in which we might situate explanations for the outbreak of these incidents; a structure which integrates both macro and micro, avoiding the reductionism inherent in both perspectives.

FLASHPOINTS

In our view the model developed by David Waddington and his colleagues in their book, *Flashpoints* (1989) provides a useful starting-point for our research. It was designed to capture the predisposing factors and triggering events in the outbreak of public disorder; to answer the deceptively simple questions of why some public gatherings degenerate into disorder whilst others, ostensibly characterised by the same constituents, do not. Of course, their model needs some radical modification if it is to help us shed light on racist incidents in schools. Waddington and his colleagues were interested in the disorders attending large-scale events: political demonstrations and industrial picketing, for instance. Our concern is with incidents which tend to be far less spectacular; they are relatively ordinary and routine – 'trivial incidents' to use the Home Affairs Committee's term (1989). Racist incidents in schools also tend to involve few, perhaps only two, participants which also distinguishes them from those outbreaks of public disorder analysed by Waddington and his team. None the less, a version of the model can be used as a lens through which we can identify and interpret the build-up to racist incidents. In the final section of this chapter we want to demonstrate the efficacy of the *Flashpoints* model by applying its variant to an analysis of those prevailing conditions (both at the macro and micro levels) which led to the murder of Ahmed Iqbal Ullah by Darren Coulbourn at Burnage High School in Manchester in September 1986. Of course, this incident was extraordinary. The murder of black youngsters by white pupils in Britain is a rare, if not unique event. But it is precisely because of its extraordinariness that we have a comprehensive and public account of the origins and development of the event: the independent inquiry chaired by Ian Macdonald and published as *Murder in the Playground* (1989) (see Hill, 1990, for a critical review of the report). But we are also persuaded by the view that the model provides the basis for incisive understandings of the dynamics of other, more routine racist incidents in schools.

The model attempts to explain public disorder by arranging events in thematic rather than chronological order. The authors insist that there are six levels of analysis which link with each other in the build-up to disorder. It is at the final, interactional, level that 'flashpoints' occur. 'The other levels may make disorder more likely', they argue, 'but its occurrence can never be taken as inevitable.' Continuing with the incendiary simile Waddington and his colleagues suggest that:

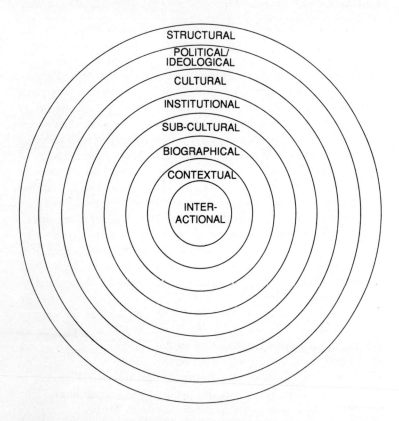

Figure 3.1 A model for analysing racist incidents in schools
Source: Adapted from Waddington *et al.*, 1989, p. 22.

To understand why a 'spark' sets off a 'fire' we need to analyse the principles of combustion. It is not the presence or absence of an individual element which is important so much as how elements fuse and interact. Our model of analysis [is] an attempt to identify not only the groups of relevant variables involved but also to specify the different levels of structuring and determination involved.

(Waddington *et al.*, 1989, p. 167)

Our version of the model comprises eight levels and is represented in diagrammatic form in Figure 3.1. The levels refer to the following:

Structural: The differential relations of power and structurally induced conflict between groups perceived as racially different in society.

Political/ideological: Prevailing systems in play at the time of the incident. On the one hand, racism: justified in terms of the current *zeitgeist*. On the other, anti-racism: defended in terms of egalitarian ideals.

Cultural: The level of lived experience and common-sense understanding within the locality and community, especially as these are refracted through the family and its networks.

Institutional: The ideologies, procedural norms and practices which are promoted, sanctioned and diffused by the school.

Sub-cultural: The children's sub-cultural worlds.

Biographical: Those factors and characteristics which are specific to the individuals involved in the incident.

Contextual: The immediate history of a racist incident.

Interactional: The actual event/incident; what was done, what was said.

The Macdonald inquiry into the murder of Ahmed Iqbal Ullah concluded that the incident was not provoked by 'racialist' motives. Ahmed's assailant, Darren Coulbourn, was not intent on killing 'someone of another race against whom he felt prejudice', according to the inquiry team (Macdonald *et al*; 1989, p. 45). On this view, of course, it might not be conceived of as a 'racial' incident, at least on the criteria and definitions proposed by some monitoring groups and agencies. However, the team members are insistent that it was a *racist* incident. Why? Because of 'the [racist] culture and context in which it took place' (Macdonald *et al*., 1989, p. 45). This corresponds with our perspective. Let us now see how the model allows an elaboration of this position by securing a tighter purchase on the constellation of background and immediate factors leading to the murder.

Structural

This refers to the salience of 'race' as an organising principle of British society. Robert Miles (1988) has coined the term 'racialisation' to denote the 'political and ideological process by which particular populations are identified by direct or indirect reference to their real or imagined phenotypical characteristics in such a way as to suggest that the population can only be understood as a supposedly biological unity' (Miles, 1988, p. 246; see also Reeves, 1983). What stems from this process is a range of practices which strengthen, and provide spurious legitimacy for ascribing differential status to the attributors and objects of racialisation: Whites and Blacks respectively. This helps to consolidate the distinction between racial and racist incidents. Put simply, racist incidents can only be experienced by those communities racialised by the white, indigenous population. It is an expression of racist oppression and cannot, nor should be, equated with other conflictual relationships which transcend ethnic lines.

Political/ideological

The Macdonald inquiry reveals that a range of ideas were in play at the time of the murder. The most obvious are the racist ideologies which constitute a deeply ingrained feature of British society. Manchester City Council's equal opportunities policy was intended to operate as a countervailing influence. However, although it embraced anti-racist perspectives it ignored the proposals of one of the Council's working parties: to include 'class discrimination' within its policy. Another prevailing set of ideas crystallised around the way the senior management of Burnage High school perceived, interpreted and implemented the City Council's equal opportunities policy. The questions which continue to tantalise are: which of these affected most significantly what took place at the school and what were the systematised frames of reference that governed the thinking of the participants?

Cultural

This refers to the parent cultures, specifically those of the white and Bangladeshi working-class communities in this area of Manchester. The Macdonald report informs us that the locality had a history of anti-'immigrant' hostility and circumstantial support for this view can be adduced from a study of race-related attitudes of white residents in this and adjoining areas of Manchester (Troyna, 1981). Another report, published by Manchester Council for Community Relations in June 1986, found that Longsight – two miles from the school – experienced more incidents of racist harassment than almost anywhere else in the city (Hall, 1989, p. 19). Of particular significance is evidence of a formidable white backlash to the City Council's anti-racist education policies. In the course of the inquiry Macdonald and his team interviewed members of the Parents' English Education Rights (PEER) group who had campaigned vigorously for the restoration of a 'good, Christian, English education' in neighbouring primary schools. The inquiry team concluded on the basis of the evidence submitted by the PEER group that:

> One gets the sense of white working class parents who have little basis on which to root their own identity and whose education has given them little or no conception of the value of their own experience as English working class and who, therefore, react angrily and resentfully to a school which, in sharp contrast to their own experience, caters directly for the needs and preferences of Asian students, thus indicating the extent to which they and their culture are valued.
>
> (Macdonald *et al.*, 1989, p. 401)

This interpretation of 'race' as a metaphor for white working-class communities' recognition of their own disenfranchisement and political inefficacy is a dominant thread in a range of recent empirical research on this subject (for example: Cashmore, 1987; Cohen, 1988; Husbands, 1983; Phizacklea and Miles, 1980).

Institutional

The Macdonald inquiry concentrated its attention at this level. The team concluded that the senior management of the school had interpreted anti-racist education in a divisive and (ultimately) destructive manner. The team members criticised the way the school had used money allocated under Section 11 of the 1966 Local Government Act; noted the absence of any adequate procedures to deal with racist incidents, such as the attack on an Asian student in the school's Careers Library in 1982; and highlighted the allegedly racist views of some members of staff. Alongside these criticisms the team evoked an image of a school where physical and verbal aggression suffused its cultural and procedural norms. As one teacher put it to the governors in 1985: 'I've taught in tough schools but this lot knocked me for six' (Hall, 1989, p. 20). There was, in the words of the committee, an 'atmosphere of violence', a description confirmed by a local inspector's report on the school.

Sub-cultural

The information which the team provided on the sub-cultural worlds inhabited by Ahmed Iqbal Ullah and Darren Coulbourn is patchy. None the less, the biographical and interactional levels of analysis provide some indication of the prevalence of racial categorisation and the normality of violence in their sub-cultural worlds. There is also evidence on the extent to which the conflict between Ahmed and Darren was a social event. Other pupils, white and black, were involved in the incident; passively with regard to their lack of intervention, but actively in terms of their role as the bestowers of approval and status. For Darren, who in an earlier fight with Ahmed had been humiliated, the reassertion of status was crucial. According to the chairman of Greater Manchester Bangladesh Association, the community is seen as comprising 'quiet, timid people, so people take advantage of us everywhere' (Hall, 1989, p. 19). As a white person living within a culture of racism, Darren Coulbourn was likely to have internalised this cultural stereotype and, as a corollary, a conception of whiteness and Britishness and the power he presumed that gave him. But Ahmed Iqbal Ullah defied that stereotype. Four Bangladeshi boys told the journalist, Malcolm Hall, that Ahmed was 'always protecting the Asian boys when they were getting hit' (Hall 1989, p. 21). According to Selina Ullah, Ahmed's sister, he was 'singled out by the English boys as a "leader" of the Asian boys' (Macdonald *et al.*, 1989, p. 12). For Darren, then, the imperative was to restore 'normality'. What was at stake for Ahmed was his reputation as 'a big strong lad' who, in the view of the inquiry team, 'did not easily tolerate injustice'. It would seem then that the public character of the confrontation was necessary.

Biographical

The decisive characteristics of Ahmed were that he was black and courageous in defence of himself and, perhaps above all, successful at school: 'bright, intelligent and good at running', according to the inquiry (Macdonald *et al.*, 1989, p. 12). Not so Darren. A member of Form 3H, a mixture of two 'special needs classes', Darren was considered to have low self-esteem as well as a long history of disruptive behaviour in the school. He had bullied and extorted money from smaller boys, both Asian and white, played truant and was regularly late for lessons. In 1985 he made two appearances in the juvenile court, once for burning down the school's Art block. His use of racist language before, during and after the fight signifies the salience of 'race' in the incident.

Contextual

There is no mention in the report of any previous interaction between Ahmed and Darren before 15 September 1986. On that day, however, they met after school at nearby Ladyburn Park when Ahmed intervened to prevent Darren bullying a smaller, Asian boy. The following day, rumours travelled around the school that there was going to be a 'fight in the park after school'. By the time the teachers had intervened, Ahmed had emerged cut but victorious. Darren was fairly dismissive of the event. He told a friend later that evening that it had been 'just a fight'. However, he added ominously: 'let him start again and I'll stab him'. The inquiry team's report begs a number of questions; above all, why did no teachers know of the impending fight and take action?

Interactional

On 17 September 1986 Darren Coulbourn went to school with a knife. He met Ahmed Iqbal Ullah in a corner of the playground where they were soon surrounded by a crowd of boys. Darren 'appeared to be avoiding the fight' but Ahmed 'was keen' and 'pushed Darren'. In the ensuing encounter Darren 'stabbed Ahmed in the stomach' (Macdonald et al., 1989, pp. 14–15). It was 8.30 a.m. He celebrated his 'triumph' by exclaiming to fourth and fifth year pupils: 'I've killed a Paki.' By the time Ahmed was examined in the hospital forty minutes later, he was pronounced clinically dead.

It is important to reiterate that neither the layout nor the way we have organised the discussion of the model implies a chronological development or linear flow from structural through to the inter-actional level. The model aims at providing a synchronic analysis, integrating macro and micro perspectives on this incident. It sets out a theoretical chain which logically links and articulates the elements of the event in a theoretical and analytical totality. It is the articulation and fusion of the different levels which produced a combustible mixture: Darren Coulbourn's fatal stabbing of Ahmed

Iqbal Ullah in the playground of Burnage High school. Only 'when conditions are propitious for disorder at every level', according to Waddington and his co-workers, is a flashpoint 'most likely to take place' (Waddington *et al.*, 1989, p. 169).

The *Flashpoints* model allows us to identify the various levels of social processes which come together in specific combinations in each racist incident, whether they are an exception, as at Burnage, or unexceptional and everyday, as in the three schools we studied. Before we turn to our own research evidence we want to develop two elements of our theoretical perspective further: our conception of ideology, and the approach we have adopted to understanding children's cultures.

A particular contribution has been made to how we understand the relationship between the macro and the micro levels of social analysis by Antonio Gramsci. One of his key ideas for understanding this relationship is the concept of 'hegemony'. The concept refers to the processes by which people's everyday common-sense understandings are shaped by, and brought into conformity with, the existing social and economic system. Questions of ideology are central to the concept of hegemony. Gramsci made an important distinction between two 'levels' of ideology. He identified 'elaborated ideologies' as the coherent bodies of thought produced and disseminated by intellectuals. Gramsci's particular concern, however, was with popular, not just 'intellectual', culture, and therefore with popular consciousness. For Gramsci everyday common-sense was 'an ambiguous, contradictory and multiform concept' (Forgacs, 1988, p. 346), composed of elements of elaborated ideologies and of notions arising from everyday experience. The concept of contradictory common-sense consciousness is central to our analysis of what race means in the cultures of children.

Hegemony should not be thought of as an accomplished state. It is always striven for, but it is also contested. Common-sense consciousness and popular cultures do not uniformly or smoothly reproduce dominant meanings. We have already indicated the contradictory character of common-sense. We are particularly concerned to identify the presence within children's common-sense of anti-racist as well as racist elements. But where do such ideas come from? How do we explain the existence in popular culture of ideas that challenge the dominant ideas in society? For Gramsci, 'commonsense is not something rigid and immobile, but is continually transforming itself, enriching itself with scientific ideas and with philosophical opinions which have entered ordinary life' (Gramsci, 1971, p. 326n). Common sense contains, therefore, both elements of dominant ideologies and elements of critical or potentially critical ideologies: 'Stone Age elements and principles of a more advance science, prejudices from all past phases of history at the local level and intuitions of a future philosophy which will be that of a human race united the world over', (Gramsci 1971, p. 324). Michael Billig and Jose Sabucedo argue that: 'commonsense, even in its most reactionary aspects, can contain the possibility of a critique of the present', (Billig and Sabucedo, 1990, p. 20). They give the example of religious notions which provide a standpoint for a critique of modern 'scientific rationality'. In the context of racism, elements of liberal discourse – discourses of 'rights' for example – may be interpreted in ways that either confirm racist discourses or provide a basis for a critique of them. We'll see this process at work in some of our discussions with children.

It would be wrong, however, to think of processes of hegemony as achieving their effects, or of encountering resistance, solely at the level of ideas. Ideologies are continuously 'put to work' and tested in social practice in everyday life. In Goran Therborn's words, 'All ideologies operate in a material matrix of affirmations and sanctions, and this matrix determines their interrelationships' (Therborn, 1980, p. 33). That 'material matrix' is constituted by the social institutions, relationships and patterns of interaction of daily life. So elements of racist ideologies gain their purchase because they are enacted in and affirmed by everyday social behaviour, because they 'work'. But the experiences of everyday life are also a source of 'sanctions'; social practices which tend to challenge dominant ideologies and give support to elements of critical thinking within popular consciousness. Gramsci's, own experience was of workers' struggles in the factories of northern Italy. He saw the basis of dissident ideas as lying in their practical experience: the 'principles of combination and solidarity' (Gramsci, 1977, p. 73) that united workers in their productive lives. The question for us is, can we identify in the cultures of children, social practices which act as sources of critical thinking and egalitarian moralities capable of offering a challenge to racism?

CHILDREN'S CULTURES

So far we have outlined a framework within which we can trace the relationships between social structures, ideologies, common-sense understandings, and individual identities. One strand among those relationships is that of 'race'. But on its own that is not sufficient to account for how 'race' works within children's cultures. We also need a conceptual framework for understanding children's relationships.

 It is useful to think of children's relationships as being constituted by three types of social processes: affect, inclusion and power. All three elements are inseparable and dialectically interrelated.

'Affect' has both positive and negative dimensions. As a social process 'positive affect' takes such forms as sharing a joke or a pleasurable experience, expressing approval, caring and sympathy. In its negative forms it ranges from dislike to hostility.

Children draw boundaries that define the micro-social structures of personal relationships that they create. They allocate each other to these social groupings by processes of inclusion and exclusion. Among the children we worked with there were two key types of social relationships: the group, which could be from three to a dozen children, and the best-friend pair. These micro-social structures were continuously being repaired and remade through interaction. Almost all the children were involved in both types of relationship. In addition, a number of them were involved in a third type of relationship, boyfriend and girlfriend relations, which we will call romance relations.

A theory of children's relationships has to be able to account for both friendship and hostility. It has to be able to explain both the dynamic towards equality and harmony and the dynamic towards dominance and conflict. The field of social relationships among children can be thought of as a network of subject positions held together by relations of social power. The relations of power are the product of two contrary social processes. One is 'domination': the assertion of the interests of the self, or of a group, over and at the expense of others. The other is 'equality': the attempt to find the fairest balance of interests among children.

The actual network of relationships that exists at any one time is the product of negotiation and struggle between many children's versions of it. Boys for example may attempt to impose an unequal power relationship at the expense of girls, who may counter it with their own egalitarian version. Arguments between friends may entail struggle over social power between them. Thus the social network is constantly changing as shifts in power change relative subject positions.

All children therefore have their own model of the social network, an ideology of social relationships, which governs the desired distribution of processes of domination and equality. This ideology consists of a complex set of elements. Some derive from 'elaborated ideologies' – for example of gender, 'race' and class, refashioned into common sense through practical experience. It includes other elements of common sense too – for example, what age differences mean in children's relationships, and the implications of friendship for processes of equality and domination.

These ideological models govern social interaction. How they are translated into interaction in any particular social episode depends upon situational factors. These would include the balance of forces – children may be less likely to attempt domination if they are outnumbered by an opposing group of friends – and the likelihood of getting into trouble from a teacher. Children develop a repertoire of interactional strategies from which they select appropriate strategies, on the basis of past experience and an interpretation of the situation, to achieve social goals derived from their 'social model', their global ideology of social relationships among children. Social models and the set of goals and interaction strategies derived from them are not of course constructed individually. They are social constructions, each continuously shaped by mutual interaction with those of other children.

We have outlined the perspective we want to adopt to explore the specific social milieu of 10- and 11-year-old children. This is a social 'region' with specific institutional contexts – the family, the school, the neighbourhood – and with distinctive cultures which embody social knowledge, attitudes and values, patterns of social relationships and strategies of interaction. Our task is to explain how, in that specific context, racism is reproduced as a popular ideology through providing children with meaningful ways of understanding and acting in daily life, how it is articulated both with existing social relationships and with other ideologies; in other words, the extent and ways in which the cultures of childhood may become racialised.

Chapter 4

Children's cultures, black experiences

To follow a class of thirty or more children through their school day is to observe a constantly changing stream of social interactions. Children in groups, in pairs, alone, working, playing, talking, laughing, fighting, displaying a kaleidoscope of emotions. The problem that is posed for the observer is to know what concepts, what framework of analysis, do justice to the complex world of children's culture and interaction. A theoretical perspective that is adequate has to be of sufficient scope and sensitivity to respond to the full range and complexity of children's culture. It has to be capable of handling conflict as well as friendship, personal meaning as well as interpersonal interaction. And, as we argued in Chapter 3, it has to be able to encompass the micro level of children's relationships and the macro level of social processes in the wider society, and explore the relationships between them.

NON-RACIST NAME-CALLING

An understanding of the cultures and relationships of the children at the three schools provides the necessary context for focusing on issues of 'race'. Much of our discussions with children was concerned with issues other than those of 'race'. We cannot present a detailed picture here of their relationships, their quarrels, the making and breaking and taking of friends, the jostling for status and self-identity. As we will go on to show, by far the most salient form that racism took in the three schools was racist name-calling. For that reason, we will begin by sketching-in the context of non-racial name-calling within which it took place. It will serve to illustrate something of the wider processes of power and ideology commonly at work.

We will use name-calling as a broad term to include both the use of negative epithets and the use of other linguistic forms having similar functions. Name-calling was a common interaction strategy used by the children. This description by three boys at Greenshire school, Martin, Anthony and Neil, gives a typical picture. Anthony said that he got picked on sometimes because he was small and Neil got picked on because he was tall.

N: And I've got my speaking problems. I had to go to have speech therapy. I spit when I talk. I get picked on because of that as well.

A: People call him 'Spit the Dog'. I get used to it because if he's talking to you and he spits on your work or something you tend to just move out the way, it doesn't bother you, whereas most people just call him names and stuff.

We asked if other children got picked on.

A: Katy and Deborah.

Int: Why Katy?

A: Because she's plump. People call her 'Fatso' now.

M: I was getting on with my work and she calls me a 'Fat Elephant' and I never said nothing and Ross goes 'You can talk' and making fun of her.

A: They make fun of Christopher because he's got chubby legs. Most of that is muscle.

Int: Why Deborah?

N: Because she hangs around with Michelle.

A: And Rachel gets picked on because she's tall.

N: We call her 'Lanky Grandma'.

M: When we were playing a game of football Deborah got the ball and Ross, before the ball came to her he was blowing it, because they keep on saying she's got fleas.

A: And Robert gets picked on because of his lips.

N: He's got big lips.

M: They call him 'Rubber Lips'.

Int: Do you think everybody gets picked on for something?

All: Yes.

N: Like some people get picked on because they've got a rubbish watch or something. Like I used to have one of these . . . [he named a type of watch]. Now it was a pretty good and nobody picked on me about that but when I got this new one nobody liked it and when Johan got one before me . . .

A: Everybody thought it was wicked because it was the first one they had seen it.

N: When I got mine people thought it was rubbish because I had it.

A: Nicholas gets picked on. He's got his little briefcase, he's brainy and he's got wicked thin legs – well Anthony has got thin legs – and we call him 'Matchstick Man'.

The boys' descriptions illustrate how name-calling serves to manage relationships among the children by contributing to the public maintenance of the hierarchical social structure of children's cultures.

What is the social meaning in children's culture of the terms used in name-calling? The wider society provides a vocabulary of terms which carry their own social weight. Clearly some are highly charged with meanings given to them by ideologies of dominance: racist terms are one category. But societal linguistic forms and meanings may be reworked in interaction within sub-cultures. In order to understand the meaning of name-calling terms we have to examine the use to which they are being put in interaction.

Name-calling entails the negotiation of social identities. Not surprisingly, as Norman Tebbit's anecdote showed us earlier, the most common type of name-calling refers to the most obvious expression of identity: appearance. As the extract from the three boys illustrates, their culture contains idealised images of male and female which provide the basis for the negative evaluation, through name-calling, of every deviation from them. Some attributes, being fat for example, already carry a negative social evaluation imported from the wider society. Others, having ginger hair for example, import no ideological charge and acquire their effectiveness solely from the interactional context.

One illustration of this is the social significance among children of apparently relatively innocuous terms. Ben and Simon, two boys at Woodshire school, were explaining how to deal with name-calling by another boy.

B: We call him 'Clacker Shoes' and that shuts him up.

S: That shuts him up that does because his name is James Clark and Clark's shoes, we call him 'Clacker Shoes' and it shuts him up.

The effectiveness of this term is not dependent at all on any societal meaning attached to it, but solely on the meaning that it is given by its intention in interaction. It is for this reason that children often categorised together terms with widely different societal evaluative meanings, as Jane does here.

• Sometimes if you swear at them they get a bit upset and say they've got a disability or something like that or they've got ginger hair and you call them 'Gingernut' they get a bit upset like that. Just things like that, things that you can make up about them.

It is because name-calling is primarily used for the assertion of dominance that apparently innocuous epithets can be experienced as hurtful. This is particularly true among friends, when they are falling out or even when the intention is playful. Philip, a boy at Hillside school, talked to us about name-calling in his group of friends. We asked him what was the worst thing that friends could do.

P: I think calling somebody is the worst.

Int: Does that happen when you fall out?

P: Yes sometimes. David calls Simon 'Four Eyes' and he comes back with 'Titch' and 'Show Off'. Then he says 'Freckles' and last year Simon and Zabeel made up funny names for each other. Simon called Zab 'Super Ted' and Zab called Simon 'Spotty'.

Int: And is that the thing that upsets people the most, being called names?

P: Yes I think so, because we don't hit each other, we just call each other names as fun, but sometimes it really hurts them and we don't realise it.

IDEOLOGIES IN NAME-CALLING

We now want to explore some examples of how elements of ideologies made available by the wider society were incorporated, and ways in which they were reworked in children's name-calling.

In the three schools, two children stood out as being subject to the greatest amount of verbal harassment. Interestingly, it was on similar grounds. Mark at Woodshire school usually came to school unwashed and with dirty clothes. He was associated with 'germs', which also had some similarity in sound to his surname. Michelle at Greenshire school was associated with 'fleas'. The connection with 'fleas' arose from an incident some time previously when it was rumoured that she had nits in her hair. The underlying social meaning of the stigmatisation of Michelle was that she was made to symbolise a social identity that the other children rejected. This imputed identity comprised two linked elements. One could be summed up as 'poor working class'. It was most frequently invoked by references to her clothes and her hair, as well as to fleas. The second was 'childishness'. Michelle was the leading member of a group of girl friends which was at the bottom of the children's social status hierarchy. The highest status group was a large mixed group of boys and girls who constantly deprecated Michelle's group for playing childish games, for not wearing fashionable clothes, and for not playing with and going out with boys. The underlying function of the name-calling of Michelle was to mark out the boundary between two sub-cultures in the classes based on two divergent and conflicting class and gender identities.

The construction and assertion of gender identities was one of the most pervasive social processes of the children's cultures. This entailed aggressive verbal and physical behaviour by some, though not all, of the boys, both among themselves and directed at the girls. Many of the girls talked to us about problems of harassment by boys, including name-calling. They distinguished these boys from others who did not harass them in these ways: there were other male identities available within the peer culture. There were virtually no reports however of the use of sexist terms by the boys. Their assertion of a particular version of male identity was accomplished through acts of verbal dominance, but not through the use of specifically sexist terms.

There was widespread agreement among the white children that name-calling about one's family was the most hurtful kind. The most offensive remarks were made either about families splitting up or family members' illness or death. Children in those situations were vulnerable to particularly offensive remarks. Hayley's comment is typical.

> When they say 'Oh your mum's done this and your mum's done that and your dad's gone, and you haven't got a father'. It really gets you up-boiled and you just want to swing at them don't you?

Kerry told us of one such incident.

> One of the children was picking on Hayley. Hayley's mum was in hospital, she nearly died, and one of the children was picking on her and saying 'Oh your mum nearly died' and it really upset Hayley.

Bindi was a boy who had told us that he didn't often get called racist names. Imran explained how Bindi had been made very upset by taunting about his mother.

> I: People started picking on him because when his mum died he had quite a lot of time off school and they went up to him and said 'Skiver, Bindi' and things like that and they asked him why he was away and he didn't want to tell anyone . . . and then at last they got on his nerves and he just said 'My mum's dead, that's why.' And they go 'Hey his mum's dead' and then they started spreading it all round the school. When he had little arguments people used to go and say to him 'I'm glad your mum is dead' and things like that.
>
> Int: Why did people do this? Is it because they didn't like Bindi as a person?
>
> I: No, they like him but when they got angry.

Robert and John told us of their experience of family name-calling.

R: I don't live with my mum and dad and I get picked on
      sometimes because of that.

Int: What do they say?

J: What amazed me was the boy that was picking on him for
      that, he doesn't have a dad. I couldn't work that out.

Int: Why would they want to say things about not living with
      your mum and dad?

R: I don't really know, they just like to hurt people really.

J: They like to have an emotional victory on somebody. They
      think they're the best at everything.

'Family' name-calling clearly draws on ideological notions of the
ideal family. But the greater part of the negative charge that such
terms carry comes not from the negative value that society may
ascribe to deviations from that ideological model, but more directly
from the evocation of personal unhappiness that the victim must have
felt at a family tragedy. The social meaning of 'family' name-calling
is not primarily imported from the wider society, it is constructed
within children's culture itself, in breach of the taboos that prohibit
similar interaction strategies among adults.

In these examples there are two types of name-calling situations.
Bindi was called names when children 'got angry'. Robert was called
names because 'they just like to hurt people'. This is a real, though
not an absolute, distinction. Gillian at Greenshire school explained
the first type. She was talking about arguments with her sister.

G: I don't know what I say to her but it's instantly in my mind
      and I just say it. I've got no control over what I say to my
      sister.

Int: Really? Is that true of things at school with your friends here
      too, that you've sort of got no control over what you say to
      them sometimes, or is it different?

G: Well sometimes I've no control over things that I think
      of.

Int: When does this happen?

G: When they start picking on me and accusing me of some-
      thing. It just comes out.

'Hot' name-calling like this occurred during heated disputes, often between friends, and afterwards often led to feelings of regret and guilt, and to apologies, though many children felt that the heated emotional state excused or justified name-calling that would otherwise have been regarded as unacceptable calculated harassment. Typically, 'cold' name-calling situations involved children deliberately teasing or harassing other children for pleasure. For many children, aggressive behaviour, verbal or physical, is *fun*, especially in the routine of school. According to Vicky, Adam, a boy at Hillside school, suffered from this.

> V: Because he's little people pick on him and call him 'Titch' and that and he can lose his temper very easily. And Adam is the one who gets into trouble instead of them.

> Int: Why do people do that?

> V: I don't know really. I think they do it so they can torment him because they know he is going to flare up, but then he ends up hurting them and goes to Mr H [the headteacher].

> Int: Why do you think they like tormenting him?

> V: I suppose it's just because they know that they are going to upset him and they love to see him upset and in a rage.

RACIST NAME-CALLING: BLACK CHILDREN'S EXPERIENCES

The black children that we talked to described racialised social interaction almost exclusively in terms of racist name-calling and related remarks. We found no instances of systematic physical harassment of black children in the three schools. In general, the black children found racist name-calling more hurtful than any other kind of name-calling. We asked Claire at Greenshire school if there were names that upset her a lot, and her answer was typical.

> Yes when they call me about my colour. Feel strongly. I don't like people calling me things about my colour, I don't like it. I feel strong about my colour.

She said, 'It doesn't really bother me about the other sorts of names, it's just the racist ones'. We asked Aina, an Asian girl at the same school, the same question.

A: I think 'Paki' upsets me a lot.

Int: Does it, why?

A: Like they're making fun of my religion. If they call me 'Paki' I sometimes tell the teacher or I just say a name back to them.

Natasha and Yvette at Woodshire school said it made them angry and want to hit back.

Int: When people here call you racist names how do you feel?

N: Feel angry. Feel like we're going to puncture their head in like and go shaking.

Y: Sometimes you feel sad and say 'I can't hit them, why can't I hit them'. I want them to hit me first . . . and Natasha's face is going bright red and your fist is like this [she clenched it].

N: Yes, my hands are shaking because I want to get my own way back.

Int: Really, it makes you angry. Does it hurt you, does it make you upset as well?

N: Yes.

The black children's experiences of being called racist names varied considerably. Some of the variation was the result of differences between schools. The most important factor here was the effectiveness of school policy, which we will discuss in some detail later. But much greater than the variation from school to school was the variation of experience within each school. Only in Woodshire school did any black children report that racist name-calling happened frequently. In the other two schools some black children reported that it happened sometimes, and in all three schools some black children said that they rarely experienced it.

The widest disparity of experience was in Woodshire school. Imran, Yvette, Natasha and Gurjit told us that racist name-calling happened to them quite often. Yvette put it most forcefully.

Y: All the time. Nearly every day I get called 'Blackie'.

Int: And is it usually by the same people or just anybody?

Y: Same people.

Int: So there are some people that you know that are likely to call you racist names and others who you know aren't going to do that? Is that right?

Y: Yes.

Gurjit had agreed to keep a diary for us. On several pages she wrote the same thing.

Why do you think people have rows? Is it because they like it or is it fighting, that's what I want to know.

She said that it was something that she thought about a lot. We asked her why.

Because ever since I have been here people have been picking on me and they have been calling me names.

She told us of a recent incident. (Her surname is Bains.)

And everybody was calling me Bains Banana . . . I just don't like it, every time when I'm at home I feel like crying, calling me Bains Bananas and I don't like it. I'm getting fed up of it now. There was one person she was calling me this horrible name starting with B . . . 'bloody bastard' and then she started calling me a 'Bloody Paki'.

But not all the black children in Woodshire school had the same experience of racist name-calling. Two of them, Bindi and Nina, said that it only happened to them very rarely. Nina said, 'There used to be, but everyone is my friend now. They haven't called me any names so far'. The last incident she could remember had occurred a term or more before.

In Hillside school, Rafaqat, Nasar, Kevin, Tariq, Nazar and Baljit all said that they experienced racist name-calling from time to time. We asked Rafaqat and Nasar if there were any things they didn't like about school. They said 'Yes, some of the children. They keep calling us "Paki"'. Nazar agreed: 'I do get called names quite a lot but not all the time'. They all agreed that children in their class did it, as well as younger children, Tariq said that friends wouldn't do it but other children might. Baljit said that it usually took place in the playground. Kevin, an Afro-Caribbean boy, told us that some boys in the class picked on him.

K: If they're in a bad mood they do. Like this boy called Robert he keeps calling me a 'Baboon', and Simon calls me the same and Aaron he calls me the same as well.

Int: Does this happen often?

K: No, not very often.

K: Can you remember the last time it happened?

K: Last week.

Only one child, a girl called Ghazala, had a different view. She said that it used to happen to her when she first came to the school three years previously, but it never happened now.

In Greenshire school the picture again was mixed. Most of the black children told us that it happened to them sometimes, and described incidents. Five children, all girls, said that they experienced racist name-calling very rarely or never.

How can we tell if the children's reports of their own experiences were accurate? First, in general the black children spoke to us quite freely about issues of 'race', whatever the frequency of their own experiences of racist name-calling. Second, their reports of their own experiences tallied closely with accounts given to us by other children.

EXPLANATIONS FOR VARIATIONS IN FREQUENCY

It is clear that racism, in the form of racist name-calling, was a part of the lives of almost all of the black children we talked to. For most of them, it was a part of their school lives as well as life outside school. It is also clear that there is a wide variation in black children's experiences of racist name-calling within the same school. These variations do not fall into simple ethnic or gender categories. In Woodshire school, for example, the two children who reported the highest level of racist name-calling were an Afro-Caribbean girl and a Pakistani boy. In Greenshire school there was one Afro-Caribbean girl, and she reported no recent experiences of racist name-calling.

How did the black children themselves explain these discrepancies? Yvette and Nina in Woodshire school were not particularly close friends and had never discussed racism together before. They were surprised at the disparity in their experiences, and agreed to discuss them together with us.

Int: How often would you say you might get called something because you are black?

Y: Nearly every day.

     [. . .]

Int: Does it surprise you that it happens to Yvette so often?

N: I never knew.

Int: Now if I asked you the same question, 'How often does it happen to you?', what would you say?

N: Not very much.

Int: Does 'not very much' mean once a week, once a month . . .?

N: About once a month.

Int: So how many times – can you remember how many times this term?

N: Never.

Int: Never? Does this surprise you, Yvette, what Nina has just said. That it doesn't happen very often at all to her?

Y: Yes.

Their first explanation was that frequency varied according to ethnicity.

Y: Probably because I'm darker.

Int: Do you think it is the case that people who are West Indian are more likely to get called names than people who are Asian, or not?

Y: Yes.

N: Yes.

In her research, Kelly does find ethnic differences (Kelly, 1988, p. 13), but in the reverse direction: Asian pupils being more subject to name-calling than Afro-Caribbean. We wondered how Yvette and Nina would explain the case of Gurjit Bains, who is, like Nina, of Punjabi descent, with a similar skin colour to her, but who reported being called racist names much more frequently than Nina.

Y: Yes because anyone can call her – like say 'Go back to . . .', also 'Bains Bananas', and she's got two names they can call her, 'Paki' as well.

N: Yes and like when they say that they get into calling her
      'Paki' as well.

Int: So you mean they start off calling her names. . .

N: 'Bains Bananas' and stuff and then they start calling her
      'Paki'. That's probably why Gurjit gets picked on.

Int: And you're saying that wouldn't happen to you because you
      haven't got names that they can make fun of like that? Is that
      right?

This answer begins to explain the discrepancy in terms of interaction
processes rather than simply skin colour or ethnicity. It is true that
some children's names are particularly susceptible to being made fun
of, and that some children seized upon these opportunities. However,
while it may be a contributory factor to the frequency of racist name-
calling directed at Gurjit, it doesn't explain Yvette's experience.

What differentiates Yvette from Nina is her much greater frequency of involvement in conflict situations. The higher the
conflict-level in a situation the more likely it is to give rise to
racist name-calling. And children who are known from previous
experience to be assertive in defending their interests are more likely
to induce aggressive behaviour in many of the other children who
come into conflict with them. We raised this idea with Yvette and
Nina.

Int: Yvette said when we talked before that this often happens
      when you have races and things because people are . . .

Y: Jealous that the other person won and they can't take it.

Int: Does that happen to you?

N: No.

Int: Why not, because you don't do races?

N: I do.

Y: Sometimes, but not very often.

N: It's just when it's big races.

Y: It's big races. Like Julie and Lisa they are determined to win,
      but for Nina and Hannah it's just a race. It's just a race for
      me as well, and Natasha and everyone, but Julie and Lisa

they just want to win each other and they just can't take it. Julie kept on winning Lisa and one day Lisa won her, and Julie couldn't take that so she breaks friends with her and I reckon she was jealous.

Int: So what I think Yvette is saying is that because Yvette is good at running races, some people get jealous of that and call her names as a result. Would you say that is true?

N: Yes.

Int: Does the same thing ever happen to you? Do you think that people call you names because they are jealous of things you have done?

N: Never has.

Int: Why do you think it's different?

N: It's not different, it's just never happened. It might, but it never has done though.

Int: But I'm wondering why. Has it never happened to you just because you don't run races and win them as often as Yvette, so people aren't so jealous of you about races?

N: Yes, because I don't much win.

This explanation is confirmed by a separate discussion we had with two friends of Yvette's: Natasha and Rebecca. They saw that the difference in how Nina and Yvette spent their playtimes had implications for the sort of interaction they engaged in with other children.

N: Yvette is more popular.

R: Nina just plays football and there's everybody lying there [on the grass], Nina is just playing football, so nobody bothers with her, but with Yvette and Natasha they are always around. They are always everywhere messing about, having a laugh, and that's when people start calling names when they've got the chance, but with Nina you can't get hold of her because she's running down the football pitch trying to get the ball.

We want to explore the idea that incidents of racist name-calling need to be understood in the context of the social interaction episodes in which they occur. In this way we can begin to explain not only variations in the frequency of racist name-calling but also variations in its social function and meaning. Before we do that we want briefly to refer to the experiences that some of the black children had of racist harassment outside school.

BLACK CHILDREN'S EXPERIENCES OF RACISM OUTSIDE SCHOOL

For many of the black children, their experiences of racist name-calling in school were one element of a wider experience of racism in their lives. Again, there was a wide variation in their experiences. Some spoke to us of incidents of racist name-calling that took place among the pupils outside the school, where they were less likely to get into trouble from a teacher. This is Bindi's experience at Woodshire school.

> B: That's when it is, outside school, because if they say it inside school they know they will only get told off, and when they say it outside school, the school can't do anything.

> Int: So who says it outside school? People in our class?

> B: Some of the fifth year. They think they are really tough and act hard and when they are outside school they start calling you 'Paki' and then running off.

Some of the black children had personal experiences of racist behaviour involving not just children outside school but adults in the neighbourhood. Zabeel, a boy at Hillside school, described his family's experiences of living in a close where they were the only Asian family. Disputes with their next-door neighbours, the Barlows, arose from the behaviour of their children.

> The people that used to live next door caused trouble and everything. They used to knock on our windows and run off and stuff and call us 'Pakis' and they used to come round. They used to blame it on us. When we swore to them they used to come round to us.

Zabeel's family got support from another Pakistani family that lived nearby.

Z: They're kind of all good friends to my dad, and the Barlows
     were causing trouble and they said 'Right we'll call loads of
     names, you call loads of names'. They called loads of names
     and there's this guy called Ajib and he's quite strong and
     Barlow ran into his own car and he didn't get out, started
     shaking, and he said 'You bring anyone here you want to,
     anyone or anything, I'll give you a fight'. He said 'OK'; he
     got out of the car and they were going to fight, he ran off
     inside, and then he didn't come out and from then on they
     didn't cause trouble, but we don't want to do that because
     if anyone causes trouble we know that we will get the blame
     for it, so it's no use for fighting. But now I realise because
     they won't stop until you hit them. If someone calls you
     names and you don't do nothing they will keep on calling
     you names until you tell them not to or hit them, that's all
     it is. Now those Barlows never have caused trouble again.

Int: And you think it was because you were prepared to have a
     fight?

Z: Yes, but I know there's no point fighting. What do you get
     out of it, nothing. You just get told off, get the blame for it.

Int: But what else could you do instead?

Z: Well you could tell the police, but what would they do? Tell
     them not to do it but they do it all over again.

Zabeel's experiences of racism in school form part, for him, of a
much broader picture. Some of the white children were aware
of this, but others had little understanding of racism in society.
Zabeel's experience of racism outside school provides him with some
important lessons which he makes use of in dealing with racism from
white children: the value of support networks among black people,
the effectiveness of force in deterring racist harassment, the lack of
confidence in the ability of authority to provide a solution, the belief
that if you appeal to them then you may very well end up getting the
blame. These are themes that we will return to.

Chapter 5

The meanings of racist name-calling

To understand the significance of racist name-calling and other forms of racist behaviour it is necessary to explore its social significance in children's interaction and the meanings it has for the white children who use it. We want to begin to examine the relationship between these two by quoting from a discussion we had with two white children at Greenshire school: Nicola and Stuart. They were talking about other children in the two classes.

S: Some of them don't like the Asian people do they?

N: They're all right. You probably talk about them and call them names, which they don't like, but then you like apologise to them or something.

S: Because you say it accidentally and hurt their feelings.

Int: Does that happen sometimes?

N: Yes, like Bhupinder.

S: I've done it before.

Int: What happened?

N: You don't mean to say it. You say something like 'Go and have a wash' or something. It's horrible you wouldn't like it but it's just like gets on your nerves, like Sandeep gets on my nerves, but I never call her names. Sometimes she's all right but sometimes she walks round me and gets on my nerves a bit, and I don't like upsetting her really.

S: I wouldn't call her names.

N: I probably would if I was that mad.

Int: When you say 'Why don't you go and have a wash', something like that, is that something that you have said?

N: I've seen loads of people saying that. From like different schools to someone, and sometimes you like feel sorry for them don't you?

S: When you get angry it just slips out. You hurt their feelings and you have to go and apologise. It's happened to me.

Int: What happened, can you remember?

S: No I can't remember, but I know it has happened.

Int: Did you apologise?

S: Yes I did.

Int: Why did you?

S: Because it's not very nice – it's not their fault that they are a different colour to us. It's just the way they were born. Older people call them horrible names. We've heard them on the telly and things like that, and we've got them in our minds and then when you get angry with them we say it but we don't mean to.

Many children spoke to us in similar terms of incidents when they had used racist name-calling. It is the racial form of 'hot' name-calling that we identified earlier. They explained that racist name-calling occurred as the result of feeling angry or upset, when it just 'came out'. Afterwards they felt sorry that they had said it, because it hurt children's feelings unfairly and was contrary to their own racially egalitarian beliefs.

A typical incident of this type involved a white girl, Angelina, and a black girl, Gurjit, at Woodshire school. Angelina was keeping a diary for us and she wrote this in it:

> Today I had an argument with Gurjit Bains in netball. She fell out with me and she kept pulling faces at me. So I called her Paki I felt bad about it but it just came out. So I said 'sorry, let's make friends' so we made friends and we played races together.

We had a long discussion with Angelina about this incident. She told us that Gurjit had called her 'pigface' and she had said 'go away Paki'.

Int: When you said 'Go away Paki', why do you think you said that rather than 'Go away pigface' or anything else you could have said?

A: Don't know. It's hard to say. I don't know really, it just came out.

Int: Has it come out like that before with other people?

A: No, because I hadn't had a very big argument with anybody before.

Int: Do you think that her calling you 'Pigface' and you calling her 'Paki' are about the same?

A: Yes.

Int: Do you think that if you had called her 'Pigface' instead of 'Paki' would that have hurt her more or less or about the same?

A: Less I think.

Int: Do you mean that calling her 'Paki' is the worst thing you can call her?

A: Yes. I don't really mind playing with people different colour from me as long as I've got a friend, but sometimes they annoy me. . . . I've got a really hard temper. When somebody calls me I go mad. . . . I think I just wanted to get my own back.

Each child chose to call the other a name that was most offensive. Gurjit chose 'pigface'; for Angelina 'Paki' was roughly equivalent but more effective against Gurjit than 'pigface'. When she says 'I don't really mind playing with people different colour from me as long as I've got a friend, but sometimes they annoy me', she means that colour is irrelevant to friendship choice, but that black children, just like white children, sometimes annoy her. In this case she turned spontaneously to the most hurtful term to get her own back, and then regretted it because it breached her own belief that, as she said to us, 'It doesn't matter what colour you are really, does it? As long as you are all right'.

Not all children regretted using racist name-calling in 'hot' situations. Some saw it as a legitimate tactic in arguments with black children. This is Katy at Greenshire school.

> K: I've called racist things. I don't call it because I'm nasty, because at the old school we didn't have any different coloured children. When I came to this school I didn't know it would be so bad. I didn't know anything about racist. I didn't know what it meant and I know what it means now, and I called Jagdeep, did I tell you, 'Bobble 07' because they wear bobbles on their heads for their religion, because he was picking on me and then I picked on him and I just called him a name.

> Int: Why do you think you called him that particular name rather than just calling him another name not to do with his colour?

> K: Because I'd heard people calling him that name and I know he gets upset about it, so if I know he gets upset about it, I call him that name.

She continued by mentioning a time when she had called Claire, an Afro-Caribbean girl in her class, 'Blacky'.

> Int: Is it different calling Claire say 'Blacky' from calling her 'cow' or something like that?

> K: It's not different, it's just a name. If there's a name about someone then you call it them. If you think they are then you call it them.

Among those children who used racist name-calling we can distinguish between those who used it as a routine part of their repertoire of interactional strategies and those who only resorted to it in spontaneous outbursts, often in heated disputes, and regretted it afterwards. This distinction between what we can call 'strategic' and 'non-strategic' racist name-calling overlies the distinction between 'hot' and 'cold' name-calling. Some children, like Nicola and Stuart, used racist name-calling only in 'hot' situations, but regretted it afterwards. It wasn't part of their legitimate interactional repertoire. Some children, like Katy, used it only in self-defence in 'hot' situations, but saw it as a legitimate strategy in that context. They had a repertoire of strategies which they applied differentially depending on context. James explained that racist name-calling was a legitimate tactic if it was used against black children who were aggressive towards you, but illegitimate against other black children. He had told us that sometimes people said things like 'chocolate' to Imran. We asked him when it happened.

J: Well he's hit you at school like and you can't hit him back at school really because you'll get the blame as well, so we just go and tell Miss and then he gets into trouble and then after school we say something and he starts calling us white names like 'Ice-cream' and things and he chases after us.

Int: What about other people, like in our class Bindi or Nina or Gurjit, do people call them names about their colour?

J: Not Bindi, no, he's nice Bindi is, I'm not sure about the girls because I don't really bother with the girls, if you know what I mean. But no-one calls Bindi it because he's nice, he doesn't do anything to you so why call him that.

Int: What about if you have an argument with him?

J: Still don't call him that. We just make friends the next day or something.

Int: Are there other names you might call him if you have an argument?

J: Well we don't say anything about his parents because his mum died in her sleep, because we don't really upset him do we. I don't know. We don't really say anything to Bindi even if we do have an upset.

Int: So what's different about Amjad and Imran that sometimes people call them names about their colour?

J: They're always at you, aren't they, they're always getting you and hitting you and they're violent and that. I don't know, but Bindi is all right, he's kind to you.

BEHAVIOUR AND BELIEFS

What is the relationship between these different racialised interaction strategies and racist attitudes and beliefs? Does the use of 'strategic' racist name-calling entail a commitment to racist beliefs?

Tricia at Hillside school regarded most racist name-calling, like other forms of name-calling, as purely instrumental, without any necessary underlying racist beliefs. Racist names were no different from other abusive terms. She had been explaining how boys might call girls 'fat cow' if they got in the way of their football game in the playground.

Int: Supposing it was Ghazala who got in the way of their game, what might they say to her?

T: They would call her a 'Paki' or a 'burnt sausage' or they'd tell her to 'get back to her own country'.

Int: And do you think that is just the same as calling you a 'fat cow'?

T: Yes.

Int: Why would they choose to say that to her and 'fat cow' to you?

Tꜱ Because Ghazala is a different colour to me.

Int: But why wouldn't they call her a 'fat cow'?

T: They don't call them 'fat cow' because they are a different colour so they can think of other names that they can't call us because we are white. Might call them 'burnt' names, 'You've been in the sun too long', but they can't call us that because we're white. They call us 'fat cow' because – don't know why but they just call us that – but they call them names because of their colour.

Int: How do you think they choose what name? Do they choose the thing that they think will upset people most or what?

T: They just say the first thing that comes into their head.

Int: If they say that to you is it because they think that all girls are 'cows' or they don't like people who they think are fat? Is that what they really think?

T: No, I just think that they say that name just so you will go off the football pitch and let them carry on with their game, because you'll just go and leave them. Sometimes they just say the first thing that comes into their head.

At the same school, Simon voiced similar views. We asked him if children who used racist name-calling really didn't like black people being in this country.

S: But when I say this, they haven't got such serious feelings about it, they just say it and mocking them and everything. They're not really serious or anything, but they really say it when they get mad or something, or whenever they see them that's what they use against them. The same with Tony, they use against him 'four eyes' and they use against Zabeel 'Paki' and if they use against David they use 'titch' or something. Things like that.

Int: So are you saying that calling somebody 'Paki' or 'go back to your own country' is just the same as saying 'four eyes' or 'titch'?

S: Virtually, yes.

Int: How do you know that although people say these things to annoy them or to get their own back or because they are angry, how do you know that they don't also think that they shouldn't be in this country?

S: The same people who call Zabeel names hang around with coloured people as well.

We asked Simon if he would use racist name-calling against, for example, Kevin, a black boy, if he had an argument with him.

Probably if I had an argument. It's something to use against him isn't it?

Several children said that people who said 'go back to your own country' didn't really mean it, they only said it because they were angry or to hurt. Kerry had told us that in that situation she might say it.

Int: Supposing the government brought in a new law that said that people who were Black did have to go and live in another country and that meant Natasha and Yvette and Nina and Gurjit and Imran and so on, what would you think about that?

K: I'd be upset because Natasha and Yvette had to go and Nina. I'd be upset because I'm their friend and I like playing with them and if I did say 'Go back to your own country' I would regret saying it. I would be really upset because I wouldn't want Natasha and that to go back and if Hayley did say 'Go back to your own country' they didn't really mean it, they were only saying it to get them back if Natasha said something to them.

Int: So supposing the people who came to take them away said 'Well look this is what you want because we heard you and Hayley saying it', what would you say?

K: That we didn't really mean it, we were just saying it to get them back, we didn't really want them to go, we were just saying it to get them back for what they were saying.

This distinction between the instrumental function of racist name-calling and its expressive function – the beliefs about 'race' that the child holds – was made by all the white children we spoke to. It was also recognised by the black children. This is Sandeep at Greenshire school.

Sometimes people say it but they don't mean it, it just comes out of their mouth.

It was Nina's view too that remarks such as 'Go back to your own country' were only said to hurt, with no necessary commitment to their content.

Int: Why do you think that people say things like that? Do you think that they really do want you to go from this country?

N: I don't think so. They just get angry inside and it just comes out and they say it.

Int: So where do they get this idea from if they don't believe it?

N: They just think of it like people say it. They hear it and they just say it. Because they get angry.

Yvette and Natasha thought the same.

N: They say 'Go back to your own country.' America or somewhere like that – a hot country.

Y: No, they say Africa or Jamaica or something like that.

Int: Do you think, I mean it's difficult to say, do you think they really want you to go away or do you think they are just saying that for something to hurt you?

N: They just want to hurt us.

Y: To get at us.

How can we explain the distinction that children make between the instrumental and expressive functions of racist name-calling? Is it simply a ritual disclaimer of racist beliefs on the part of white children, a rhetorical strategy used in reporting racist behaviour? Or does it represent a real ideological disjuncture and contradiction?

Teun van Dijk (1987) has analysed the strategies of conversational discourse about 'race' used by white people. He notes the characteristic form of 'I'm not racist but . . .'. He explains the contradiction as one between the speakers' real racist attitudes and their desire to create an impression of not being prejudiced. These strategies of self-presentation and impression-management serve the function of persuading the listener by presenting the speaker favourably as rational and unprejudiced.

In a discussion of van Dijk's ideas (Billig, 1988b, p. 96), Michael Billig notes his distinction between

'the effective expression of semantic macrostructures [themes]' and the 'interactional and social goal' of creating the desired impression in the hearer. He goes on to assert that 'these two different sets of goals may be sometimes in conflict: a direct or "honest" expression of the beliefs or the opinions from the speaker's situation model may lead to negative social evaluation of the speaker by the hearer'.

(van Dijk, 1983; p. 384)

Billig argues, rightly, that for van Dijk this is a contradiction *between* ideology and interactional strategy, not a contradiction *within* ideologies themselves. But for Billig, interactional strategies are themselves ideological, and therefore the conflict embodied in 'I'm not racist but . . .' is one 'within individuals, who have two contrasting ideological themes on which to draw. To use Althusser's (1971) terminology it is this ideological contradiction which "interpellates the subject" ' (Billig, 1988b, p. 97).

Billig's conceptualisation of the interactional domain as itself ideological is an advance over van Dijk, and here we can refer back to our earlier discussion of Gramsci's concepts of elaborated and common-sense ideologies. In the context of children's culture, the interactional repertoire is governed by ideologies of social morality and social identity which both draw on elements of wider societal ideologies and are continuously reaffirmed and reshaped in social interaction.

We want to develop this distinction between what Billig refers to as thematic ideologies and interactional ideologies in two ways.

First, we want to develop the idea that the two ideological domains, the thematic and that of interactional strategy, are independently variable. Billig and van Dijk only explore one possible variant: racist beliefs combined with non-racist interactional strategies. But if we translate this model from 'secondary' episodes of accounts of 'race' given to researchers to 'primary' episodes of racialised interaction – in our case to racist name-calling by children – it opens up another possible combination. Here the interactional goals, and the ideologies in which they are embedded, are very different from the van Dijk/Billig scenario. The interactional goal is not to persuade the listener that one is not racist, but to achieve offence and hurt by using racist terms. This interactional ideology may be associated with thematic ideologies of 'race' which are racist, or which are non-racist or anti-racist.

Second, the concept of ideology allows for the possibility of inconsistency and contradiction. Billig notes this in warning against the frequent practice of social psychologists, uncomfortable with notions of cognitive or attitudinal ambivalence, who impose a unitary model of consciousness by claiming that one attitude is more deeply held and therefore is the 'real' attitude. Billig uses this idea to discuss the contradiction between a racist ideology, regarded as unitary, governing attitudes and opinions about 'race', and ideologies of rationality, which he derives from liberal themes stemming from the Enlightenment, governing accounts of 'race'. But he doesn't address the possibility of *anti*-racist elements within discourse, and therefore of contradictions within ideologies of 'race' themselves. Nor does he pose the question of contradictions within ideologies of interaction.

The model we are proposing to account for racist name-calling (and by extension other forms of racist behaviour) locates racist name-calling incidents in relation to two axes. One represents the user's beliefs and attitudes to 'race', ranging from racist to anti-racist. The other represents the user's interactional repertoire, and ranges from racist to non-racist. Individual children may be more or less consistent in both their 'thematic' attitudes and their interactional repertoire.

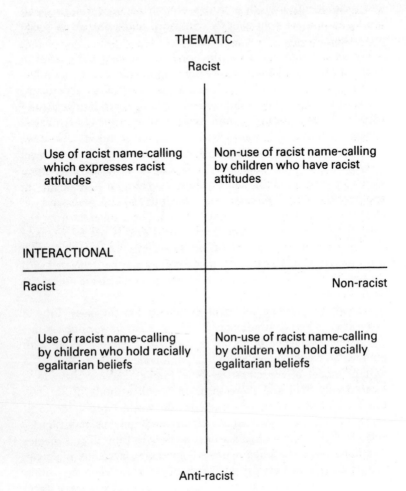

Figure 5.1 A model for locating racist name-calling

Our point is therefore that the existence of racist beliefs cannot be simply read off from incidents of racist name-calling, any more than racist beliefs automatically generate racist name-calling. Society makes available to children a powerfully charged vocabulary of racist terms, but their use, while trading on the negative meanings that they bear, does not necessarily imply a commitment to the racist ideologies from which they derive. Each incident of choosing to use racist name-calling (whether 'hot' or 'cold', strategic or non-strategic), or of choosing not to use it, needs to be concretely analysed to determine the specific combination of the two dimensions of behaviour, thematic and interactional, which it represents.

We are not saying that non-expressive racist name-calling, i.e. the use of racist names by children that is not expressive of racist beliefs, is not racist. We would argue that it is racist in two other senses. First, it is a form of hurtful discrimination against black children. Second, it trades on a racist frame of reference and thus tends to reinforce its legitimacy within children's culture. Just because an instance of racist name-calling was understood as not expressing underlying racist beliefs doesn't make it any more acceptable to black children, as Parminder made clear at Greenshire school:

> If somebody called me a name like 'Paki' or something, why don't they tighten their mouth right, they should have been thinking what they were saying. Whether they said it on purpose or not. You should think what you are saying.

THE ATTITUDES OF WHITE CHILDREN

The emphasis in the extant literature, as we saw earlier, is on the range and intensity of racism amongst white children. This often forecloses analysis of white children's anti-racist positions. Yet in our study we found that many of them echoed the position of Sarah at Greenshire school.

> Underneath it doesn't matter what colour skin you are. You've got skin, you've got blood, you've got bones, you're just ordinary children, you're just the same, 'cos if I had brown skin I would still be the same person, but with just a different coloured skin.

Gemma belonged to a large group of girls at Woodshire school. 'Most of our gang like black or other different kinds of people. We don't mind what colour they are.'

However, many children, black and white, acknowledged that some white children, perhaps a minority, perhaps a majority, had racist beliefs. By far the most common explanation given by black children, like Kevin at Hillside school, was to do with 'belonging to this country'.

> Int: Why do you think so many white people think like this and behave like this?

K: Because they think this is their country and that we should go back to our own country. Like they say to Pakistanis.

Int: How would you answer somebody who said that?

K: I would say 'This is my country just as well as yours because I was born here'.

Int: And do you think that would convince them or would they still think the way they thought?

K: They would just say something like – it wouldn't convince them I know that. . . . It's just because of my colour. I was born here but they still think that I wasn't, but the only thing that changes it is because of my colour.

Mandeep, a girl at Greenshire school, saw the relationship of prejudiced attitudes to a history of domination. 'White people, they think they're better than coloured people. They think they rule the world, but they can't.'

Most of the white children agreed that some white children had racist beliefs. There was a range of explanations suggested. Stuart at Hillside school said:

Well they don't like other people coming to England and because they keep coming and bringing their families and they are trying to make a living in England, and most white people can't buy shops because all the other foreign people have, they start thinking that they are all going to come to invade them, and they start calling them names and telling them to go back to their own country and make up jokes about them.

Ben at Woodshire thought that 'They just think it's not so good to be brown. They think white is better'. Simon added 'It's just like some men think they're better than women. I think it's just like that'.

Some children thought that the cause lay in cultural conflict. Tina at Hillside school said that

Some people don't like the food they eat, some call them names because they read the Koran and we read the Bible and some people just call them names because they talk different languages and they go 'Bud, bud, bud' and try to do languages.

Stuart at the same school thought that some white people didn't like black people 'because of their skin. It's a different colour', but also because they were envious of black culture. 'They've got different cultures and stuff like that, and probably white people are jealous of it. So they make up names.'

Racist views were not expressed to us as an explicit and elaborated statement of principle in the way that anti-racist views often were. We do not believe that the reason for this lies in the research situation, in other words that the children had coherent racist views which they might elaborate among themselves but not to an adult. We found no evidence that such exchanges of views took place. Expressions of racist views were generally partial and fragmented, and to a great extent context-bound and embedded in social interaction. They were often combined with expressions of racial egalitarianism. It is our view that this accurately reflects children's consciousness. In the next chapter we will illustrate this in more detailed case-studies of three children. Before we do that we want to examine some examples of typical social processes of children's culture in order to explore the ways that they may become racialised by both interactional and thematic ideologies of 'race'.

ACTING TOUGH

One of the most common explanations that children gave for racist name-calling was that it was motivated by the desire to 'act tough'. This was a term mainly ascribed to boys. 'Acting tough' was part of the interactional repertoire for establishing a particular type of male identity through the assertion of dominance. This is Nasar's explanation at Hillside school.

> N: Because they think they'll look good. They think they're the leaders and they can beat everyone.
>
> Int: And they're trying to prove it are they?
>
> N: Yes.

Many of the white children agreed that this was a common motivation for racist name-calling. In this example, Paul, also at Hillside school, rejects our suggested explanation in terms of racist beliefs in favour of one in terms of interactional processes of dominance.

> Int: People who call black children names to upset them, do they do it because they think that they are better than black people?

P: They think they're tougher. They think 'Well being as I'm acting tough everybody thinks I'm tough, so I can go and call anybody a name'.

At Greenshire school Nicholas and Jagdeep also thought that racist name-calling was governed primarily by interactional ideologies of 'acting tough', independent from a commitment to racist beliefs.

Int: Do you think that they think that because they're white they're better than you, or is that nothing to do with it?

N: They might think it but I don't think – they might think it. It might cross their minds but I don't think that really has much to do with it.

Int: Really? So what does have to do with it?

J: Acting tough.

Acting tough was a common male cultural trait, but it was not restricted to boys, as Raj and Nicholas illustrate here.

Int: When he calls you racist names, or other people do, why do you think they do it. What is in their head?

R: Think they're tough and everything.

N: 'Oh look at me I'm the toughest in the class.' 'I'm going to tease him and get him really worked up.'

Int: But you said that Michelle had called you those names. Was she doing it to show how tough she was or was she doing it for another reason?

R: The same, to show off in front of her friends.

Several children at Greenshire school made the point that some children took pleasure from hurting other children, and their use of racist name-calling was part of a general pattern of behaviour. This is Tracey.

Int: Are there some people who do this, or do all the white children say these things, or just some of them?

T: Some people that pick on everybody does. People who like picking on anybody they can see, anybody they want to pick on, they pick on them. Sometimes they even pick on their friends, they don't realise who they are talking to.

There was an incident at their school in which Dian, an Afro-Caribbean girl, had tried to borrow a rubber from a white boy called Colin and he'd said he only lent it to white people. We were talking with Dian and two white friends, Lee and Scott, about the incident. They saw it as an instance of Colin's more general disposition, not restricted to racial conflicts.

Int: Why do you think he said that?

S: I don't know, it's just the kind of person he is.

L: He likes upsetting people, he thinks it is a good laugh to upset somebody.
[. . .]

L: He loves hurting feelings.

D: Because he can upset coloured people except he doesn't hurt white people emotionally, he hits them physically, because you could just be walking along and he'll just do a fly kick on your back, and it really hurts.

CONFLICT BETWEEN OLDER AND YOUNGER CHILDREN

Many children described patterns of conflict between younger and older children. This is Simon at Hillside school.

Int: And what about how older children and younger children get on? Do they more or less leave each other alone or are younger children always annoying older children and older ones sometimes bullying younger ones?

S: Exactly. Younger children always annoying older children and in that case the older children start to kick them down. It's the only way of retaliating – well it's not the only way but it's the way most boys react. Say if a first year came up to you: 'Oi fatso come here'. 'Come here and say that' I'd say. They would come up to you: 'Fatso' – whack.

Int: Why do the younger children do this?

S: They're trying to find out how tough you are and they just want to annoy you for the fun of it.

Int: Is it always the older children who are reacting to this and the younger ones who start it, or is it sometimes the older ones who start it?

S: Sometimes the older ones.

Int: So might they do?

S: Pick on the little ones. Say one of the little ones is walking around with a bag of crisps, one of the older ones will go whoosh and catch it, and hold it in the air and the first year will jump up and catch it. Things like that happen a lot.

Through this ritualised conflict between older and younger children the status hierarchy of children's culture is continuously made and confirmed, and their social identities shaped. When there were black and white children involved, the process often became racialised, though the primary motivation was itself not racist, as Bindi recognised.

B: Not many people say it to me. Only the little kids say it.

Int: Why do they do it?

B: Don't know.

Int: I mean are they just trying to annoy you or what?

B: Probably. Like little kids they like people chasing them, don't they?

It seemed to be only younger boys who harassed the older boys, but both younger boys and younger girls harassed the older girls. At Woodshire, Hayley and Rebecca were talking about a group of girls in Year 4 (i.e. 8/9 years old) and Yvette, a black girl in Year 6.

H: Rosa she thinks she's tough. She had a go at me out there so I pushed her back and I goes 'Stay away from me because if I hit you I'll hit you more than you could hit me' and then Rebecca pulled her away and then Yvette was standing there and she goes 'Stop it Alison and Rosa' and she goes 'No I won't Paki, golliwog'.

R: They're like a gang.

H: They think they're tough.

The process of challenging and maintaining the status hierarchy between the age group also took the racialised form of racist name-calling as a means by which older white children dealt with harassment by younger black children. David explained that 'if they come up to you and torment you' the sixth year boys will sometimes say ' "Go back to your own country" or something'. Two white girls at Hillside school, Victoria and Marion, described how they used racist name-calling as a way of dealing with harassment by Asian girls in years 3 and 4 and the distinction they made between them and their close friend Baljit. This is Marion:

> I think younger children get called quite a lot as well because once they were disturbing me and Baljit so they kept calling us names – not horrible names but they kept disturbing us when we were trying to play, a gang of them came. So we started calling them little names and then they started getting worse so we had to call them Pakis and then they shut up. But they caused that themselves because Baljit doesn't do anything to deserve that but they were just getting on our nerves. We were trying to play a game and they just kept disturbing us and Baljit and they wouldn't let us do anything, and we told the teacher and she told them to go away. We went up the other end of the playground and they just come again.

ASSERTION OF ETHNIC IDENTITY

The assertion by black children of their ethnic identity produced both positive and negative responses on the part of white children. For example, at Greenshire school Mandeep told us about how children had responded to her wearing Indian clothes. She said that she only wore them to school on special occasions, for instance if they were doing a topic on India. When she and her friends wore them for a Bhangra event, 'they go "I like your suits" and all that. Like nearly all the girls said they like it'. Mandeep said that girls and boys 'said the music was good. Like Nicola she joined in. If we had all Indians in it, it would be sort of like racist, and we put some English people in it'.

But she said that wearing Indian clothes also provoked some hostile remarks. 'They sometimes show off, yes. Say if we wear this suit like, with some buttons to it and a top like. We wear them and they say "English clothes are better" and they say "From Indian it's chronic, all those things".

The context of remarks like these was competitive personal interaction. As we have argued, the power of racist beliefs lies in their ability to make apparent sense of everyday life. In a kind of self-fulfilling prophecy, they receive continual reinforcement through their use as an interpretive framework. Episodes of personal interaction are explained by elements of racist ideologies, and in turn serve as further proof of their validity. For example, each instance of assertion by black children can be located in the interpretive framework supplied by racist notions of national identity and black people 'taking over'. In the following discussion Samantha, a girl at Greenshire school, responds in this way both to an assertion of black cultural values and to a simple act of assertion that has no connection with 'race' other than that the boy who does it is black. The negative evaluation she gives to his act of attempted dominance is racialised into further evidence for her negative evaluation of black people. We were talking about a discussion we had had previously.

Int: You said 'This morning Mandeep who is on the same table as us and Parminder they kept on saying Indian songs are better than English songs'. Why were they doing that?

S: I don't know. Suppose because they're Indian and we're not so they think that theirs is better than ours but it's not. We don't understand theirs, they understand ours. They do some in PE. I'd rather do country dancing though.

Int: 'And I thought like saying "Well why do you come to live in this country then, it makes me mad" ' you said.

S: Yes, because if they think theirs is better than ours then I don't know why they bother living here. I'm not that racist but I like some Indian people but I don't like others. I don't like Parvinder because he really acts like he owns the country. He tells you what to do. I got the microscope the other day and he took it off me. He looked at it and he wasn't using it and I took it off him and he goes 'Oi that was mine' and goes and tells Mr A [the class teacher] that I've got to give it him back. That's what gets me mad about him.

The expression of Asian cultures that provoked the greatest amount of comment from white children was the use of Asian languages. Parminder at Greenshire school explained that

> I nearly always in class talk in Indian to Mandeep or anybody else. Sometimes to English people I go [she spoke in Punjabi] something like that – that means 'Come here' to somebody. If they're English they don't know what I'm on about sometimes.

Katherine, a girl in her class, said that this made her feel like saying racist remarks.

> They're always speaking Indian and you never know what they are talking about. You say 'What are you talking about?' and then they start swearing to us in a different language and we're going 'What are you saying, what are you saying?'

The competitive character of children's culture, with its constant pressure on children to maintain themselves in the face of attempted dominance, led children to interpret the use of Asian languages as a possible dominance strategy. There was a rational element in their belief. Rafaqat at Hillside school described how when he played with Pakistani friends in the playground they usually spoke in Urdu in order to exclude and perhaps provoke white children, 'Because they don't know what we are saying then if we speak Urdu'. This sometimes led to bilingual exchanges of verbal abuse.

David, a white boy at the same school, thought that using Asian languages gave children an unfair advantage in another way:

> if they're getting done and you're getting done they can walk away and say something to the teacher in Pakistan language like a swear name, and the teacher won't know what they are saying, but if we said it they would know what we were saying and then we would get done.

The views of David, Katherine and Samantha are not necessarily primarily motivated by racist beliefs. The key process at work here is at the level of the culture of interaction, which is governed by a relatively inflexible principle of equality. The ever-present threat of dominance makes children very sensitive to any perceived breach of the equality principle. The consequent uneasiness that they feel about the use of Asian languages follows from this. For some children, like Katherine, it coexists with a belief in racial equality.

For others, however, like Samantha, any assertion of ethnic identity reinforces the racist beliefs that she holds.

RACIST REMARKS BEHIND THEIR BACKS

A form of racist behaviour that we have not so far considered is remarks between white children which black children are not intended to hear. While these serve the interactional function of reinforcing inclusion, they may also reveal underlying beliefs.

Baljit, a girl at Hillside school, was explaining that she wasn't called racist names very often. She said that it hadn't happened at all that term. Her two white friends, Marion and Victoria, joined in the discussion.

> M: They did behind her back last week. They started calling you names when you had gone to the teacher to ask about your maths, they started looking at your book and saying horrible things like 'Look at the Paki writing' and things like that, because she's got a different sort of writing.

> V: She writes big and me and Marion write really tiny.

The following account by Katherine at Greenshire school reveals both racist belief and behaviour among her friends and her own ambivalence.

> K: Well most times I don't call people racist names now because for one thing if my mum found out that I was saying racist names she would absolutely kill me, because my mum has got a best friend and she is black and I really, really like her, and so I didn't really say racist names very often. It's just if they really got me mad and things. I didn't really call people racist names. I didn't say it in front of their faces, if you know what I mean, I said it to Nicola and all them lot and those lot say it, and I felt like saying to them 'Just pack it in because you wouldn't like it' because I can remember when Kirsty, Gillian and me were going round, this was the other day, and I just stopped doing it and Gillian and Kirsty carried on, because I didn't like what they were saying. Because we were talking about – I don't know what they were talking about, I just heard them talking because we were all working together and Gillian and Kirsty were talking. And then they started saying 'Let's all have a packet of brown shoe polish'

and all this stuff. They started shouting 'A barrel of brown shoe polish' and then Dian started singing it and she's black and she didn't know what they were talking about at all.

Int: Were they talking about people in our class?

K: No – I know what we were talking about! Esther, my friend, her auntie has just got married to a black man and they're going to have a half-caste child and I was saying that I think half-caste children are dead sweet, and then they said 'I don't think they are when they get older' and I said 'I think that they are' and they started saying 'A barrel of shoe polish'.

For black children who became aware that their friends might make racist remarks behind their backs, it put into question the nature of their friendship as well as their apparent non-racism, as Zabeel found.

Int: So you thought that people had stopped calling you names?

Z: Yes then after that I heard people call me names. Like say Mark makes fun, say a Muslim or an Indian can't talk very good he goes '. . .' [Zabeel put on a mock-Indian accent] and he makes fun and then he goes 'That's a bit like Zab'. I don't want to hit Mark and then after he's a good mate. And one day Paul, there was these Muslim girls, and the ball went over there and he never knew I was there because if I was there he wouldn't have called them anything, and he said 'Hey you niggers pass me the ball' and when he saw me he goes 'Oh oo, I never said it to you Zab'.

Int: And that was Paul. He's another of your friends?

Z: Yes he's my friend but you see, I don't know if he's my friend or anything because behind my back he just calls the Muslims, my friends, names. I don't get it sometimes.

Zabeel's apprehensions that there was a climate of racist attitudes among some of the children in the class, including some of his friends in the group of boys, received some confirmation from remarks made to us, separately, by three children in his class (and not made by children at either of the two other schools). Tricia told us:

T: Ghazala came to my house one day and she stayed to tea and she went home about 7.30 and people started calling me names the day after because she had come round to my house.

Int: Did they? What did they say?

T: They said I'm a 'Paki lover' because Ghazala comes round to my house and we play. They say horrible things and say if I want to play with them I should have been a different colour, I shouldn't have been the colour I am.

Int: Who said these things?

T: Tony, Liam. Because everything Tony says Liam agrees with him. I think if Tony wasn't there Liam wouldn't bother about them.

Int: So what did you say to them?

T: I just told them not to be so stupid. I just say 'Well I'm not that colour am I. You don't have to be their friends if you don't want to but I am,'Because Jennie feels the same way as I do, she's not bothered about their colour.

Independently, Stuart, a boy in her class, said the same thing. He had been giving his own views to us, which were decidedly anti-racist, but he said that he hadn't talked to other children about them.

S: No, kept it to myself up to now, because other people think I'm going dotty because I like black people more than I do white.

Int: What other people think that?

S: Lots of people probably. All the big kids, they all think they are horrible, and just keep thinking about themselves and not other people.

EXCLUSION

We have said earlier that friendship relations among the children showed little evidence of being affected by ethnic criteria. Friendship groups were often mixed. Black children often had close best friends who were white, However, there were all-white friendship groups, inevitably so because of the small proportion of black children. We found it difficult to tell if racial exclusion was a factor in the composition of these groups, though we found no evidence to that effect. Exclusionary processes within a group which are not the result of explicit decisions by group members, and which are not accompanied by any expression of racist opinions, are extremely difficult to identify. We cannot say that no such processes of silent exclusion, based on shared tacit, and perhaps unformulated, understandings, were at work. None of the black children, who were generally perceptive about racist undercurrents in children's relationships and behaviour, made any mention of exclusionary practices either experienced by themselves or directed at other black children. We would also note that many of the white children were quite perceptive in their interpretations of other children's attitudes, and the absence of statements by white children about black children being excluded by white children from activities and relationships is also indicative.

There were two areas where there was some evidence of processes of exclusion at work. The first was among the younger children. We have already noted the reports of racism among the younger children. Further investigation of this was beyond the scope of our study, but the following remarks by Gemma at Woodshire school indicate the existence of exclusionary processes. She was talking about the racial equality in her group of friends, and we asked if there were other children who didn't think like her.

G: Yes, sometimes because when I go and call for them and I'm playing with Yvette and Natasha and people like that, they go 'Oh I don't want to play with them because they're brown.'

Int: Really? Who says that?

G: All sorts of people in the school, but not in the class, not in our year group. All sorts of people say that 'cos I called for this girl who said 'No I don't want to play with Yvette or Natasha, 'cos they're brown'. So Natasha and Yvette got very upset.

The second area we wanted to examine was that of boyfriend and girlfriend relationships. The existence of strong patterns of sex-segregation among children is well-known. One factor that reinforces them is the desire to avoid being taunted about having a girlfriend or a boyfriend. But this is not the whole picture. Much less attention has been paid to the existence of cross-sex relationships among children, and virtually none to 'romance' relationships. Yet these are significant features of children's culture at this age.

The frequency of cross-sex friendships and romance relationships varied across our three schools. It was least in evidence at Hillside school. But at Woodshire and Greenshire schools there developed during the year a distinct sub-culture among some of the children, based on new types of relationships between girls and boys. In both schools a mixed group of boys and girls emerged who played and hung around together in school and who shared activities outside school, going down town, or to the cinema, or the youth club, or just hanging around. Within these groups romance relations grew up, ranging from close friendships that had lasted for months to a merry-go-round of ephemeral liaisons. Talking about romance – who fancied who, who said and did what – joking about it, manipulating arrangements, occupied much of their time, especially that of the girls.

This new sub-culture represented a new differentiation of the social identities of the children in the top classes. Far from making these children the subject of taunts, romance relations were a source of high status within the class. Cross-sex and romance relationships signified 'growing up', achieving greater independence, moving from childhood to adolescence. Romance relationships opened the way that could lead eventually to adult identities of marriage and parenthood. The question we wanted to ask was to what extent were the children's romance relationships, and their conceptions of their future identities, racialised.

We found some evidence of exclusionary practices on the part of some children, and also subtle processes of sub-cultural differentiation among the children that may have opened up a process of divergence for some children along ethnic lines. There seemed to be three racialised patterns within the romance culture. First, a certain segregation along ethnic lines. We found little evidence of romance relationships between black and white children. Second, less involvement in them by Asian children than by white children. Third, the children least involved of all were Asian girls.

The reasons for this were complex. Some white children said that some white girls and boys would not go out with black children.

Anthony explained why white girls were not as attracted to two Asian boys, who were among the leading members of the mixed-sex group at Greenshire school, as they were to white boys.

> Yes, because of the colour of Raj and Par, they're the strongest, it's just because of their colour. If they were English like we were and were white then people would tend to go for them more because they are the strongest and if they were white it would be a lot better.

Some white parents had expressed disapproval of their children going out with black children, as Leanne explained.

L: I've heard like Nick he's not allowed to go out with coloured people.

Int: You say that Nick isn't allowed to. Who by?

L: His mum says 'If you come home with a coloured person . . .'. Because his mum's dead racist.

But white children did not necessarily agree with or act in accordance with their parents' racist views, as Nicola shows.

Int: In your group people are all friends and some are black and some are white. When it comes to boyfriends and girlfriends, does it make a difference there, do you think?

N: No, because I like Raj. Like we were mucking around and saying like the top ten who you liked. He would probably be my third. I would go out with him if like I asked him and he said 'Yes', I wouldn't really care if he was Indian, but my dad don't like me going out with Indian people. He just don't like them.

We asked Stacey at Woodshire school if people in the two top classes were more likely to fancy people who are the same colour. She answered 'I fancied Amjad once. It doesn't make any difference to me'. She then went on to talk about mixed marriages.

S: I know these people who live opposite me and their kids are called Leroy and Angelina. And their father is a dead-tall black man, right, and the mother is a white short person, and so they're black. I find it a bit weird and my mum went on to my uncle and said 'A white woman can't marry a black man' and then my uncle goes 'Yes they can if they

> want' and they had a big argument.

Int: Why do you say you think it is a bit weird? Do you not agree with your mum about this? You agree more with your uncle?

S: I agree with my uncle, I don't really mind, it's not my business what people do. I don't mind if black people marry white people.

Int: So why do you say it's a bit weird?

S: It makes no difference because if you imagine they were white, it wouldn't make any difference would it? . . . It's not that weird, I can't explain the words for it.

Stacey's remarks illustrate that both views are represented within the local white community. It is difficult to know what she meant by 'weird'. Perhaps the most likely interpretation is that it reflects the contradiction between her ideas of racial equality and the persisting hold of a social norm based on 'same-race' marriages. It was noticeable that children, in discussing which children would make suitable boyfriends and girlfriends for each other, tended to automatically use ethnic criteria. The roots of this categorisation system were not necessarily specifically racial: it drew on wider, idiosyncratic notions held by some of the children that similarity in appearance was an indication of compatibility. For example, Sarah, talking about white girls and boys, thought that 'if they've both got the same coloured hair they stick with each other for quite a long time, but if they're like different coloured hair then they suddenly change'. On the same grounds, one white girl was thought to be a suitable partner for one Asian boy because she was quite suntanned. For some children, differences in appearance between children of different ethnic groups in the class inevitably became assimilated to these notions of natural affinity based on appearance. But it seems likely that this was compounded by notions of a social norm of 'same-race' relationships. This was derived from two sources which seemed to mutually confirm each other. One was their own experience, in the family and the community, that the majority of relationships were 'same-race'. It was simply 'how things are'. The second was ideologies of romance made available by commercial youth culture, within which mixed-race relationships are still very much the exception.

Ethnic-related patterns in romance relationships also received reinforcement from the choices that black children made. Some of the Asian girls were opposed to having boyfriends, not just now, because they felt themselves too young, as some of the white girls also said, but as a general rule laid down by their parents or their religion. Aina foresaw a divergence among her friends when they were in the secondary school as her white friends 'went off with boys'. But some of the Asian boys did have girlfriends, even in opposition to their parents, as Sundeep admitted.

Yes, I've had one even though my parents don't let me. It's against our religion. We don't really go out with girls, but I went out with her.

The only Asian girl who had boyfriends was Bhupinder. For her, the freedom to have boyfriends if she wished was part of a more general rejection of the authority of her traditionally minded grandparents who brought her up, that led her explicitly to disavow her ethnicity. According to Parminder, 'Bhupinder, she wants to be English. She goes "I wish I was English" '.

Among the Asian girls, their perceptions of their future romance relationships lay within their ethnic group, not necessarily only because of their realistic recognition of factors at work excluding them from other relationships, but because of positive cultural choices. For Parminder, who secretly fancied Parvinder, language was important. She said 'I wouldn't really marry an English person because I can speak Indian and they might not be able to', and this would be important because she nearly always talked to her Indian friends in the class in Punjabi.

These complex processes of 'race', culture and gender give rise to contradictory dynamics of social differentiation and integration within children's cultures. The dominant process seems to be one of divergence along ethnic lines. Especially in schools with a majority of white children, the emergence of a romance culture among white children may serve to undermine existing friendship relations between black and white children and marginalise some black children from the dominant sub-culture. But cross-'race' romance relationships, where they exist, offer a powerful rebuttal to processes of racialisation within children's cultures. It seems likely that these contradictory processes will tend to be amplified as the children move into secondary schools and mainstream youth cultures of romance become increasingly salient.

RACIAL NAME-CALLING BY BLACK CHILDREN AGAINST BLACK CHILDREN

A number of incidents of racial name-calling by black children against other black children were reported to us. These were in general quite isolated incidents. At Greenshire school, for example, only one instance was reported. There was one exception to the infrequency of these incidents, and that was Amjad and Imran, two notoriously aggressive twin boys at Woodshire school. The most frequent target was Yvette, an equally assertive Afro-Caribbean girl. Names used included 'blackie', 'nigger' and on one occasion 'black slag' (the latter was virtually the only instance of sexist abuse that was reported to us in any of the three schools).

How are we to explain the use of racial terms of abuse by black children against other black children? Any analysis that bases itself on the idea that racist name-calling is invariably the expression of racist beliefs must inevitably explain this in terms of the internalisation of racist values by black children. Our approach, which makes a variable connection between the instrumental and expressive functions of name-calling, does not necessarily require such an explanation. It may be the case that Imran and Amjad's remarks to Yvette expressed racist views that they as Pakistanis held about her as an Afro-Caribbean, but that cannot simply be read off from their use of such terms. Certainly when Amjad called Yvette a 'Paki', as Hayley reported to us, we do not need to conclude that he had internalised a negative image of his own ethnic identity. On the contrary, our conversations with him and his brother revealed the opposite. We would rather explain it as part of his interactional repertoire, trading on racist societal ideologies, but entailing no belief-commitment to them.

We want to focus on one incident involving Amjad and Imran, together with the three boys who shared Imran's table: Bindi, a Sikh, and two white boys, Simon and Richard. It illustrates how racist taunts, in this case saying 'Salman Rushdie', may be set in circulation and taken up both by black and white children. This is Bindi's account.

> Well Imran caused it. We've got these ten gods in our religion. They are special gods and he started saying things to me so I called him 'Salman Rushdie' and he offended me and I couldn't

take it so I offended him back. Then Richard and Simon they got it off me and they started saying it.

Simon confirmed: 'And that was how it all started and before we all got told off we were all saying "Salman Rushdie" if he offended us.'

What did all this mean to Imran and to the two white boys, Simon and Richard? The starting-point for understanding the actions of Imran is that he shares with his twin brother Amjad the reputation of being the toughest boys in the school, a reputation which they continually try to prove. Bindi said that one of the starting-points of the Salman Rushdie incident was Amjad 'acting tough'.

He said that he could beat me and Pardeep up really badly. . . . He said he could probably beat anyone up in the school and he kept saying it and I think some people started laughing so when we got outside I just started calling him names because he started.

It is very difficult to say what part the experience of racism plays, and has played, in Imran's compulsion to act tough. But we can identify two factors. The first is that Imran does experience racist name-calling from other children, as we have already seen, and being tough is effective in both responding to, and deterring, racist name-calling. But in addition to their experiences in school, the brothers also have a whole set of experiences of racism that they and their family have been involved in outside school. Those experiences belong to a social context, the adult world outside school, in which attributes of toughness are necessary for survival, as Imran described:

I: My dad owns a shop down town, it's games and pool tables. In there when I play on this game people asked to lend it, but I said 'No' and they said 'Paki'.

Int: Who said that?

I: This boy called Chris. He said it to me because I didn't lend him 10p to play on this game. They started calling me names. . . . He took me and my brother down the alley and he started having a fight with us and so my brother went back and got a hockey stick and was fighting with him.

Int: Really? What was this other lad fighting with you about?

I: It was over 10p 'cos he wanted 10p off me and I said 'No' and then he started getting jealous and calling me names, and then these kids took me down this alley and got me in the corner and started hitting me in the corner, I had a bruise on my head, and my brother went back and got a hockey stick and he hit him with it.

Int: And these other lads, were they all white?

I: Yes. Seven of them.

Imran also explained that sometimes 'They write "White power" and things like that' on the shop. Whatever the exaggerations there may be in his account, it clearly refers to a realm of experience that white children have not directly experienced, and that many white children of his age have no awareness of.

For Simon and Richard, 'Salman Rushdie' was valuable as a strategy to compensate for the habitual dominance of Imran.

S: He was quite upset and so now every time he offends us or any one of your friends, we used to say 'Salman Rushdie' to him. In a way to get our own back and also to keep him away because then he would keep away from us for the day. He is quite a strong boy, he is stronger than anyone else in this class and the whole school and so we get on with him as a friend but if he tries to hurt us, he probably does because he is very strong, so we were all saying 'Salman Rushdie' to him if he started to offend us.

The taunt of 'Salman Rushdie' has a different meaning for Simon and Richard and for Imran. Two different but overlapping frames of reference are in use, and Simon and Richard on the one hand and Imran on the other are positioned differently with respect to them. For Simon and Richard, the dominant frame of reference that governed their actions was that of the historical relations of power within the group, specifically the dominance of Imran. For Imran that frame of reference was highly salient, but it was significantly different in two respects. Firstly, for Imran it was of much wider scope. He was already involved in competitive power relationships with secondary school boys and in the adult world of his father's shop. Second, racism for Imran meant a whole set of experiences specific to him, partly because he is black and Muslim and they are white and not, but also specific in that he has experiences of racism in the world outside school (the fight in the alley) which are beyond the horizons of the two white boys' worlds.

Chapter 6

Case studies

In this chapter we are going to explore in some detail the views and behaviour of a number of white children. The first four, David, Robert, Adam and Jacky, reveal something of the interplay between elements of racist ideologies circulating in society and the ways in which they are taken up within children's cultures, and in particular how they are put to work in social interaction. The remaining ones, those of Gemma and Tina, Jane, Karen and Charlotte, illustrate the understanding that some white children of 10 and 11 years of age have of racism, and their commitment to racial equality.

David

We begin with David, a boy at Hillside school. We had several discussions with him. He was a member of the group of boys which included Zabeel. Our first discussion took place with David and another member of the group, Paul. We had asked if children ever said things like 'Go back to your own country'.

P: Yes. That subject is brought up a lot. Like 'We don't want you here'. 'You're in the wrong country.' Most of the names they call are because they are coloured.

Int: How do you mean?

P: They might call them 'Paki'.

Int: Why do you think they say 'Go back to your own country'?

P: Because they think that being as most white people here, they don't want them there because they've got their own.

D: Well this is our own country isn't it?

P: We don't own it. We can't say 'No we don't want them people, they'll have to stay'. Like when Vietnam people come over on the boats they got sent back, didn't they. I think that is why they got sent back because they didn't want them in that country. They thought 'We've already got enough, we don't want any more. We're going to send them back'.

D: We don't really want that many more here do we because they take over, don't they? They have all the shops and everything.

P: Yes, all the corner shops.

D: I wouldn't mind if they didn't do that, but they do.

P: They get away with more things than white people I think.

Int: Like what?

P: Pickpocketing probably. They probably blame it on somebody else. That other person will believe them.

D: Yes, I mean, black people can call white people names in their own language, but we don't understand what they are saying do we?

P: I read in the papers quite a few weeks ago now that there was this black man and he was walking around with an 18-inch knife and then a few weeks ago I read it, and there was the bloke walking around with this little boy about that big and this white bloke he got put in jail and the black person got away with a warning I think, or a fine.

Int: And are you saying that that was unfair and the black person wasn't treated the same as the white person.

D: I think a coloured is more dangerous.

P: No, I think they're about the same.

David and Paul introduce three of the most common themes of children's racist beliefs: black people are taking over the country, they are given unfair advantages, and they are associated with

violence and crime. We should also note though that their views
are not identical, and that there is a dialogue and a movement of
ideas as they work out their stances in the discussion.

We had a subsequent discussion with David on his own. We asked
him about his idea that black people 'get away with more things'
than white people, and again he drew on his experience in peer
interaction, this time referring to bilingual children being able to
'say something to the teacher in Pakistani language like a swear
name, and the teacher won't know what they are saying, but if we
said it they would know what we were saying and then we would
get done'. His conclusion is that 'at home they should talk in their
language and at school and things like that they should talk in ours'.
This is a strategy of generalising from the interactional level to the
societal level similar to that used by Samantha earlier. Real instances
of relative disadvantage in interaction serve to exemplify elements of
racist ideologies of black dominance in society. An appeal to equality
in peer interaction is used to justify inequality.

We wanted to explore his ideas about 'taking over'. We asked him
what he meant when he said 'We don't really want many more here
because they take over, they have all the shops'. First he referred to
his experience of Black families, mainly of Pakistani descent, moving
into the area where he lives.

D: Well they build places up like say there is this street of
      Whites and then one White moves out and one moves in,
      and then they come in next to each other, so they are all
      together like that.

Int: And do some people not like that?

D: No, because when you walk past the house it smells, and
      what they are making smells, curry and things.

Int: And is that not nice? Do some people not like that?

D: Well it's a horrible smell.

Int: What other reasons do people say that they are taking
      over?

D: Because when they have families they have about six or
      seven kids.

Int: Do people think that if there are more black people that
      would be a bad thing?

D: Well it wouldn't be such a bad thing, it would just be like there would be too many.

Int: Why would it be too many?

D: Because there would be more of them than there would of us.

Int: And people would think that that should be a bad thing? Why do they think that?

D: I don't know, probably because they will be more than us, like prime ministers, soon there might be a black one and so on, and then they will be ruling us, and then instead of our Christmases and that making a song and dance about it, there will be theirs.

David is able to recreate some common themes of racist discourse – moving into white neighbourhoods, large families, smell of cooking – in terms of his own experiences. In another discussion he added another.

We used to live next to black people and when somebody died – because our entry came off theirs as well – and when somebody died millions of them came down the entry and we just couldn't do with it, so we moved.

The very specific personal experience of the blocking of the side passage of his house by mourners in a different cultural tradition serves as a symbol of the process of 'taking over the country', just as Christmas serves as the embodiment of the cultural tradition that is seen to be at risk. What explanation does David give for why black people want to 'take over' in this way? He thought that black people were more likely to favour black people than white people, and white people were more likely to favour other Whites, and that was 'normal'. We asked him what white people might do. 'They might have a big riot so they don't rule us. They would probably have a war and whoever wins gets this country, but I doubt it.' His final remark signifies his recognition of the unlikelihood of this scenario, but the logic of his thinking is clear.

One of David's friends was Zabeel. David, and other boys in the group, said that they didn't use racist name-calling within the group, 'Because it isn't fair. We're probably a different colour to them'. This ability to adopt a black perspective was also revealed when we asked him how he thought Zabeel felt about being called names by children outside the group.

D: I don't know but I bet he wishes he weren't here.

Int: Really. How do you mean?

D: Wasn't in this country.

We then asked David what he would say if people said 'Well look we don't want Zabeel and his family living here, there are too many of them and they are taking over and they should go away'. Would he agree with that?

D: No.

Int: What would you say to them?

D: I'd say 'Why not they haven't done any harm really'.

Int: Supposing they said that they are taking over and they are taking over all the shops and things like that.

D: I don't know, it's a hard question that one. It's probably because he's my friend and I don't want him to go away because then I would be a friend less and he won't make me laugh any more.

Int: Right. Do you mean that what you said goes for other Pakistani people but not for Zabeel because he's your friend and that is different?

D: Yes because Zabeel is different. He joins in with our things, like the things we do as well. Most Pakis don't.

David recognises the logical contradiction that he is in, but resolves it with the argument that Zabeel is different because he joins in with white people (which of course, solely in terms of David's experience, is true, since Zabeel is his friend and other Pakistani children aren't). David's understanding of 'race' contained two strands. One was the ideas he had about racial conflict in society (presumably echoing his parents' ideas), and made concrete in his interpretation of events in his neighbourhood. The other was the de-racialised culture of his friendship group and his friendship with Zabeel. The conflict was resolved by the strategy of 'refencing', of making an exception.

Robert

Some of the children we talked to thought that there were some children who seemed to get pleasure from hurting other children, and for whom racist name-calling was one strategy in a repertoire of harassment. It was invariably boys who were placed in this category. Perhaps the clearest example in the three schools was a boy called Robert at Greenshire school. Robert was notorious for his aggressive behaviour and had been in trouble on several occasions for racist name-calling. We asked him about it.

> R: Oh yes, I call them 'Niggers' or 'Pakis' or 'Chocolate biscuit' or something like that. They've got a lot to put up with. If you've fallen out or something and you see something brown or black you go 'Oh look there's your cousin over there', like that.

> Int: Does this upset them or annoy them or what?

> R: Yes.

Neil, who knew Robert well, described him like this.

> He's one of those people that don't like black people. He's about the only person that all the black people in this school don't like. There's a few white people that don't like the odd black person, but it's only natural to not like one person. It's just Robert, he hates every black person. He doesn't mind some of them, like Rajvinder, he plays football with him. But he doesn't really like Rajvinder that much either.

Neil and his friend Martin told us of a recent incident

> N: Jagdeep, it was in like circle time when we talk to each other, because we used to watch these films called 'You and Me' and we was watching about boys and girls and name-calling and Robert goes up to Jagdeep and calls him 'Paki' something, 'Bobble 07', and Jagdeep starts crying and tries beating him up.

> M: Jagdeep gets told off.

There are two points here – the way that a racist incident was provoked by an 'anti-racist' lesson, and Martin's perception that the black child got into trouble (along with Robert) – that we will return to in Chapter 8, when we look at responses to racist incidents. Here we want to focus on Robert himself. What did 'race' mean to him, and how can we explain his racist behaviour? Without such an explanation, there is a danger that boys like Robert are simply pathologised as racist bullies.

Robert's interaction with other children was characterised by aggression. As Neil said, 'Robert is always picking on somebody'. Sometimes it was younger children. Robert described how 'the little ones' had footballs and 'we kept nicking them off them and tripping the little ones over. I loved it'. Katy told us how Robert and another boy picked on girls.

K: Yes they pick on anyone really. They just come up and kick you and call you names. They'll just do anything for no reason. They'll just come up and kick you, whatever they please. They're that kind of people, you know, just want to show off. . . . What Robert is going to be at Community School I don't know. There's going to be lots of fights if he carries on like this at primary school, he's going to be in a really bad state, be one of those people, you know, muggings on the street, because he is really bad like that.

Int: Why do you think he does it?

K: Just to have fun because he just likes doing it. It's his way of doing things. When he's bored he thinks 'Well I'll go and do this to the girls' or something.

Physical power and aggressive violence were central to how Robert saw his own identity. On one occasion we asked him if some people liked arguing.

R: Yes, like me. I love blood and violence, I love it. Where you get all blown to bits and that lot, and you see all the flesh fly in the air and hearts and like that.

He went on to give a detailed description of violent scenes in the film *The Predator*.

R: Then when Arnold Schwarzenegger – my best hero, and then it's Rambo – well then he goes and rips him apart. He chucks him against a tree and rips his heart out and then chucks it down. Then, you know Arnold Schwarzenegger – I've got posters of him everywhere haven't I?

We asked him if that was who he would like to be like. 'One time I will be', he said. He told us that his father did body-building, and his mother and he used to too but they couldn't afford it anymore. He believed it was important for boys and men to be tough 'so if you have any wives you can protect them', ''cos the men are the man in the house', 'they're in the boss's shoes like of the house'. He was against any reversal of traditional gender-roles 'because it just looks like the women are better. Because the women are more gentle'.

The image of Robert so far is that of an extreme stereotypical macho male. His next answer though suggested that it did not correspond fully with reality.

Int: Do you think that is true in our class, the boys are tough and the girls are gentle?

R: Some of the girls are tough, they'd rip your head off. One punched me in the face.

Int: Really? Who did that?

R: They didn't, but they would. So I punch them in their face.

There is an indication here of the element of fantasy in Robert's world-view. It was clarified by some remarks that Neil made.

N: Robert is not exactly very tough, and people pick on him a lot so he has to start on them and when they start on him they just kind of hate him for the rest of his life. Sometimes he says 'Sorry' and things like that but it's hardly ever he says it.

Int: When you say he's not very tough . . . I mean if you talked to Robert he always says how he likes fighting and how tough he is and how he fights people and all the rest of it. Have you heard him talk like that?

N: Yes, he thinks he's tough but I think he's a fourth year [i.e. year 6], he's only just a fourth year because he's younger than me. And all the third years pick on him a lot and when he has scraps with them he always gets beaten up. Like Jagdeep when that fight happened, Robert was nearly crying then. Jagdeep is always beating somebody or other. Jagdeep is just like Robert. He's not as bad as Robert sometimes.

Int: Does Robert hit girls as well as boys?

N: He hits people like Kirsty and Nicola and the group with Ross, but he wouldn't hit anybody else.

Int: Why does he do that?

N: Because he's a part of the gang and Ross picks on him and so do the girls sometimes. Not as bad as the boys.

Neil explained that Robert wanted to belong to the mixed group of boys and girls, of which Ross was the leading boy, which was the highest-status group in the two top classes, but that Ross and other members tried to exclude him.

Some weeks later we had another discussion with Robert during which he revealed another side of his life. He said he got depressed.

Int: Why do you get depressed?

R: I don't know.

Int: Because you have problems or because you're bored or because . . .?

R: Yes I'm bored and problems.

Int: Both. What sort of problems do you have?

R: I keep thinking about my dad because he's left home. That's one of my weaknesses. Things I haven't done with my mum and things I have done to mum, like swear to her and that lot. I feel guilty about that. Feel sorry for myself, and that's it.

Int: Why do you say thinking about Dad when he left home is one of your weaknesses?

R: Because people make fun of me when they've got their dads.

Int: Do they?

R: That's one of my weaknesses and it gets on my nerves wicked bad because I just punch them and kick them. I'm using a lot of punches – I punch everybody.

Int: Who picks on you because of that?

R: Neil, this Indian Rajvinder, Sundeep, sometimes Jason and other people that can kick me in. And this little nigger at this school – because he's a dumb little – I can't swear anyway –

he's dumb. That's what I think and everytime I see him it's always round his house because he's got a ginormous brother that goes to the Community School. He's about a third year and when I go he'll probably be about a four and a half year.

Int: Are you saying this little lad calls you names, does he?

R: Yes, 'rubber lips'. That's what really gets on my nerves.

Int: Is that what he calls you?

R: I call him 'nigger'. Probably because I'm riding past and I'm quite far away from him, that's why I call him, and today I'm going to kick his face in when I see him because he called it me yesterday.

We asked if calling names like that meant that he didn't really like black people very much.

R: Well I do because a few days ago on Friday some friends of mum's asked us round for tea. I didn't like it but I said I liked the chappatis but I didn't like them either. . . . We watched telly. Mum and the lady and the man talked while Pindy, Jagdeep, me and Nic [his sister] went round to them. We went there at 6.15 and left there at 12.30.

Int: Is that the first time you've been round there?

R: No, because their mum used to look after me and Nic and then after a while Mum used to look after Pindy and Jag.

We realised that the incident in the class between Jagdeep and Robert took place in the context of a history of friendly relations between their families, based on shared child-care arrangements between their mothers. Wanting to probe further into Robert's attitudes, we then asked him what he thought of the school's firm policy on racist name-calling.

R: That's right. It's a good rule and it's fair, because you shouldn't call – it's not allowed to be called white people or black people any names. Jason got done all the time for calling names. You get a red card.

Int: But you call people racist names sometimes.

R: Yes, and I get a red card. If you don't get a red card you get a letter sent home.

Int: If it's a good rule because it's wrong to call racist things, because you said it was wrong to call people racist names, why do you do it?

R: Probably because I'm in such a rage I forget all of the rules. Forget everything. My only quest is to bust that person's hand.

Int: So when the rage has gone down, how do you feel when you have done something like that?

R: Guilty. Well not guilty, sad, I wish I hadn't done it. Well they start it usually, don't they?

Int: But what can you do then, when you've called them something and then the rage has gone down and you feel guilty or sad?

R: No, just sad that they started or I started it. Wish they hadn't.

Int: Why do you wish you hadn't?

R: Well if I'm still in a rage I'm glad, but you know when Miss G [the headteacher] tells us off, yes, and I'm still in a rage, well I've got an excuse then because it's in my mind. It's like an on-button. It's like a timer and you've got at least about three minutes to be all raged up, and then when the time has gone you're back to normal again.

Robert's racist behaviour is part of his overall aggressive style of 'being-in-the-world'. We can only guess at the unhappiness in his family life that lies behind it. The macho male fantasy, exemplified by his film heroes, provides him with a limited vocabulary of social skills which are inadequate even in their own terms to enable him to negotiate the world of peer culture. They trap him in a self-fuelling cycle of aggressive conflicts with other children which lead to failure: he often loses them, other children dislike his aggressiveness and exclude him, he is constantly in trouble with teachers. His beliefs about 'race' seem to be largely the product of, and mobilised by, his fantasy-led aggressive interaction style. Whether they have any independent existence apart from that we cannot say, but we would point to the elements in his life that offer at least the potential of a contradictory perspective: the relationship between his family and Jagdeep's, his positive evaluation of the school's anti-racist policy, and not least his own ability to recognise the gulf between his fantasy and the reality of his life.

Adam

Adam is a white boy at Hillside school. He is very small, and has got into a lot of trouble for reacting violently to other children when they make fun of him. He and Zabeel are friends, though not close, and Adam is not a member of the group of boys that Zabeel belongs to. He told us about racist name-calling:

> A: It's like if you call them a different colour, it's like saying 'You don't belong here, you belong somewhere else with your colour'. Like that, like you're sending them away.

> Int: Do you think that people do belong with their own colour?

> A: No, I'm not bothered.

Later we asked him to explain what he meant.

> A: I mean I think it would be quite a good world if people were mixed up. I reckon it's everybody's world. It's not just our world, it's their world as well. I don't mean that people have to go to Pakistan – black people have to go to Pakistan – and white people just stay in England. I reckon it ought to be a mix up, because it's their world as well as our world. As long as they treat it well.

He then went on to explain the instrumental function of racist name-calling

> A: Well I mean if somebody says like 'Go back to your own country', the Asians have got to do something to make them really angry before they can say that. I mean I wouldn't say that unless they did something to me and made me angry. But I've just thought that is one of their weak spots. That is another one of their weak spots if you say 'Go back to your own country, you don't belong here'. That's their baddest weak spot.

> Int: Why?

A: Because they, I suppose, they know that they don't really mix.

Int: I don't quite understand. You said that you thought it would be best if anybody belonged here and everybody was sort of mixed up, but you said also that sometimes you might say 'Go back to your own country'.

A: Well if they got me angry, I would.

Int: Does that mean that you would want them really to go back to their own country?

A: No, I don't really, it's just that that's their weak spot. It just gets me so angry and I say that, and I don't really mean it. If I say that – I said it to Zabeel. He's got me so angry in the end I've said 'Sorry'.

Adam explained the incident. He had been writing and Zabeel had kept mocking his writing and nudging him.

Everytime I tried to do better he kept on nudging me, so in the end I got so angry that I said that to him. After school I said sorry, I felt really guilty because I said that and I didn't really mean it.

So far we have presented Adam in terms of a contradiction between his stated non-racist views and his willingness to use racist name-calling to retaliate against black children's 'weak spot'. We now want to examine his views on 'race' in more detail. Perhaps his remark that 'they know that they don't really mix' is an indication that his own views are not consistently non-racist.

Adam told us about a group of Asian children in the top class in the previous year. 'Nasar he used to be really bossy and he used to go around causing trouble in a great big bunch, all of them in a great big bunch, just going round stirring up trouble, beating everybody in for nothing'. They 'just wanted a bit of fun I suppose. Liked seeing people cry. But I didn't take it. Every time he hit me I just punched him back because I just wasn't taking it'. Adam was particularly vulnerable to harassment because of his size. But now they have left. 'Nasar was the strongest Asian in the school, but now there's nothing to compare to what Nasar was. They've all gone down, and we've gone a bit up.' We asked what he meant by 'we'. 'Well what I mean is like us, our colour, because they used to go up and start beating everybody in but now it's gone like down and we've grown a bit.'

From this account we want to pick out two points. First, Adam's vulnerability to tougher boys, including Asian boys whose own display of toughness might be at least partly the product of experiences of racism as well as being a phenomenon of male assertiveness. Second, the high salience of toughness and of 'race' for Adam as categories of social cognition. The playground hierarchy is understood in terms of a combination of a racialised 'us' and 'them', and a hierarchy of toughness.

This association of 'black' and 'violence' was a theme that ran through Adam's ideas about 'race'. Immediately after his account of Nasar and his friends, he began to tell us a story about a man called David who lived in the flats that he used to live in.

A: He used to be really, really kind, but one day I went round knocked on his door, the door came open. I went in and went in the living room, looked around for David and he was on the sofa. He had been cut down his cheek there and there and he had all a bruises all over his face because of these two Paki men who came round and I don't know why, but they just started beating him in. They've always done that. They've always run away, jumped over a wall. And I told my mum and she came round. She phoned the police.

Int: How does that fit in with what we were just talking about?

A: Well it just proves that if they don't control themselves while they are this age, when they grow up they are going to be even worse.

Int: And are you saying that that is especially true of Pakistani people or true of anybody?

A: Well I suppose really anybody. . . . I suppose it's like mugging, something like that. So I suppose really it can just prove how they can get really vicious when they grow up if they don't stop beating other people up. You see things on the telly. They take it for granted and think 'Oh I'll do that at school'.

Int: Who do you mean by 'they'? Do you mean especially Asians?

A: Yes, Asians.

We asked him what he meant by 'seeing things on the telly'.

Well films like people going round in their language they are saying – not in English, their Pakistan language – and just like films, like kings. There is a king sitting there and he orders his men to go and kill somebody and starts bossing them around and using them as slaves, so I suppose that is what they think.

We then asked why he thought Asian people were more likely to behave like that than white people.

I suppose it's their mums' fault really. Mr H [the head] sends loads of letters to their mums and he says 'I want this letter back and if it's not back intact, I'm going to go round and see mum'. It comes back and it says 'Dear such and such, your son is behaving very badly at school being a great big bully. If he does not pack it in in the next few days we will expel him from school'. And then the lady will sign and most of them just think it is not very good and it gets put in the bin, so they never get back.

He added that this had happened to Zabeel, and the mention of his name reminded him of another incident, one that had happened some two years earlier.

A: Now I did a very stupid thing once. We were outside and I was playing about with my brand new penknife and I was stripping a tree down with a metal bar and Zabeel came across the road with his great big brother. I don't know why, I just ran. I went 'No – my penknife'. I ran straight outside and got it and opened it up. I just got so angry I just lost control. I opened it up and said 'Leave me alone' and I folded it back up, put it in my pocket and just went upstairs. Told my mum about it though.

Int: What did they do that made you take out your penknife and say 'Leave me alone'? Did they do anything?

A: They started pushing me around. This was when I was living in the flats. They will only do it when we are outside school. They never do it inside.

We asked who was involved in this incident.

A: A few others from this school, but there were some white ones as well, and it was Zabeel's friends.

Int: So were they all boys?

A: Well there were three that were girls. There were three girls and too many boys. But the one when I got my knife out was a little one. He was with them and he's in this school now. Going like this thinking that he's all brave and that, and this girl came rushing up to him and she was just about to hit me, and that's when I got my penknife out.

Int: Really. She was going to hit you, the girl?

A: Yes. Because really I suppose Zabeel told her to or somebody.

This must be one of those 'critical incidents' that embody significant elements in children's lives. It was obviously a frightening experience for Adam, and not an isolated one but representative of many experiences of harassment that fill Adam's life, in which his small size is an important factor. (Perhaps it is also relevant that his parents have split up and he doesn't get on with his mother's new partner. 'Me and me dad have turned out worst enemies – I don't know why.') Personal experiences of harassment involving Asian children are interpreted in terms that reinforce racist schemas linking black people and violence, for which he finds further evidence in the David incident and the image of king and slaves from an Asian film on television. He is able to explain the connection between child and adult violence in terms of lack of parental control, and here he draws on his own experiences of complaints being made by the headteacher to Adam's mother about his own violent outbursts.

It should be noted that Adam often qualified the racist implications of his remarks. For example, after he had recounted the incidents we have referred to we asked him if he was saying that Asian people were more liable to violent behaviour.

A: No. I'm not saying every single Asian goes around beating everybody in. I mean we wouldn't be in a very nice world then would we? What I'm saying is some of them do. I reckon more white people do it than Asians. But I suppose David did something wrong to make those Pakis get on to him.

We interpret this as more than a rhetorical disclaimer of prejudice. They are evidence of his efforts to arrive at a fair resolution of the tensions in his thinking between racial egalitarian views and racist constructions.

Jacky

We want now to discuss in some detail the views of Jacky, a white girl who was a member of the large group of girls at Woodshire school. The discussion begins with her account of a racist name-calling incident between her and Nina, an Indian girl in the same group, that took place over a year before, and explores her views about 'race' that underlie it.

I think I said 'Why don't you go back to where you come from' and just called her a 'Paki' and she called me an 'Ice Cream' and a 'Blob'.

Jacky is quite a large fat girl. We asked her why she had chosen to call Nina 'Paki'.

She called me 'Ice Cream' which means fatty, then I just thought well she's not fat so what can I call her, well she's black so I'll call her 'Blackie'.

Afterwards they made friends. In a separate discussion we asked Nina about the incident. She saw it as probably not reflecting any underlying racist beliefs.

Int: Why did Jacky call you a name? Is it because Jacky doesn't really like Asian people, or . . .?

N: She is nice to me like. She does take me swimming and stuff. She's not bad but she just called me the name, probably because we were having an argument and we were just calling each other names and she called me that.

Int: You mean that she probably doesn't really think that?

N: She probably didn't mean it.

But is it as simple as that? Jacky told us that she and Nina often had arguments.

Well me and Nina aren't close. We always argue. We always have loads of fights. We're still friends but we're not close friends like all the others are.

The arguments with Nina were more serious than with others in the group. Among the other girls, they managed conflict by walking away from each other before the argument escalated to name-calling.

When me and the others start fighting we just break up, but me and Nina carry on. Like I think that if we don't carry on Nina will think I'm a chicken, because if you walk off from Nina she goes 'Chicken, chicken' and starts calling you that, so I don't walk off her. But when I'm with Hannah we just walk off together, and Jayne, because we know that we are going to really fall out, we just separate, and then after a few hours we make up again.

The failure of the normal de-escalation technique may have been due to a more aggressive approach that Nina took in arguments. Other girls in the group criticised her to us for being too dominant. But the causes of the conflicts lay deeper, in the competition for relationships among the girls in the group, and Jacky's fear of exclusion. This is Nina's explanation.

Int: Is Jacky a friend of yours?

N: Yes, she's one of my best friends but I don't get on well with her. Well none of us get on well with her.

Int: Why is that?

N: Because if we start walking together and talking to each other and telling each other secrets she starts crying. I don't know why but we say 'We'll tell you after' and she just goes 'Well I'm not your friend' and she starts crying.

Int: Is that because you're leaving her out of things?

N: Well we weren't leaving her out, we were just talking to each other and she thought that we were leaving her out.

Int: Does this happen quite a lot?

N: Yes.

Int: Is that because she'd like to be really best friends do you think, more than she is at the moment?

N: I think she wants to be more than any of us.

Jacky reveals her insecurity with friendship relations in the group in her remarks about her relationship with Hannah, her best friend.

J: When she is with other people I think she tends to be really hard. When she's on her own she's really nice. And that is when we mostly fall out, when she is with somebody else and we are in a group of three or four, because she starts just laughing like all the life that is shut up inside, and then when other people go away she just opens the gate and she's nice again.

Int: When you say she is hard, what do you mean?

J: It's like when she is with people, not her mum or dad or her brother, when she is with her other friends, just like she changes. Like she gets a hard coating on the outside like gates, and then when she is with me she just opens the gates and cuts the hard coating and she's nice when she is with one person. . . . When I'm with Hannah I feel more relaxed but when I'm with a group of people I feel that I have to do things right or they will laugh at me. When I'm with one person I know that I can trust Hannah, I just feel all right.

In this context, how does Jacky explain why she and Nina don't get on?

J: We've just got nothing in common at all.

Int: How do you mean you've got nothing in common, like what?

J: Like I'm fat, she's thin. I'm white, she's black. She doesn't do anything that we do. She doesn't listen to music. She likes Bros group and we all hate it. She plays football and we don't. She just doesn't do anything that we do. We talk about boys and all she can do is talk about football.

Int: I don't see how her being black and you being white – what difference does that make?

J: Well she just doesn't like the same things as we do. She likes to play more with people of her own colour I suppose. It's not being nasty or anything but she just likes to play with people more. She plays with Gurjit a bit and she just plays football with the boys – her own colour. She plays with white people but not as much as she plays with black people. I think she feels that she can trust them more than white people.

Int: Why do you think she feels that?

J: Well because if like I said, if we have an argument we can call each other names but if she has an argument they can't call her black because they are black as well.

Jacky develops a complex argument here. They don't get on because they have nothing in common. Among the things that separate them is ethnicity. This is different from the other factors, Jacky implies, because it is one-sided: it is Nina who makes ethnicity an issue by preferring to play with children of her own colour. But there is a good reason for this: it's nothing to do with 'cultural differences', it is that she can trust black people more because they don't call her racist names. 'Race' provides an explanation for why they don't get on, but in fact neither the accounts of other children nor our own observations support Jacky's view that Nina prefers playing with

Black, or Asian, children. On the contrary, Nina's best friend for
over a year, with whom she was very close, was a white girl, and
Nina was one of the most popular members of the large group of
girls in her class, the rest of whom were white. She did regularly play
football at playtime, but most of the children who played, mainly
boys, were white.

We wanted to find out how Jacky understood racist name-calling.

Int: Do you think she feels that when people say things like
       'Blackie' to her that they are saying it because they think
       that white people are better than black people, and so she
       doesn't feel that she can trust them.

J: Yes I think so.

Int: And when people say to her 'Go back to your own country'
       she feels that that is different from calling someone 'Fatty'
       or 'Skinny' or 'Four Eyes'?

J: Well most of the time people start calling her 'Blackie' so I
       think it is the same as me, she starts calling them names as
       well.

Int: Do you think being called 'Blackie' is the same sort of thing
       as being called 'Fatty'?

J: No because I think it hurts them more because it hurts Nina
       because she was born in England and it's just her mother
       and father are Asian, but she was born here anyway.

Int: So do you think she thought when you called her 'Blackie'
       and 'Go back to your own country' that you meant that this
       was white people's country and black people don't belong
       here and they weren't as good as white? Is that what you
       meant when you said it?

J: Well at the time, yes, because I thought she was born in
       India, but she told me that she was born in England and
       I said 'Well I won't call it you again' and I haven't called
       her it since.

The distinction between black children born in this country and
black people born abroad is important for Jacky. You can't say
'go back to your own country' to children born here, but you can
to others. What was the significance of this distinction?

Int: Do you mean that you think that black people who weren't born in this country should go back to where they were born?

J: I suppose so, yes, but I like some of them. It's just that some of them I don't feel right when I'm with them.

Int: Really, how do you mean?

J: I feel on edge all the time and that I can't talk to them.

She is describing her relationships with some black children in the same terms as she expressed her insecurity with her friends. We asked why she felt this was, and she qualified her remarks.

J: Well Jasmine, she's Asian I think, I can talk to her a little like but she's fun to be with. Some of them are fun to be with but it's the ones that are really mardy or don't like doing things that I don't get on with. I get on with most of them.

Int: Are you saying that ones that are mardy and so on you think they shouldn't live in this country?

J: No, I just think I should leave them alone and let them get on with whatever they want to do, but if they come near me I won't talk to them or anything.

We returned to her point about 'going back to their own country'.

Int: What I'm wondering is then what you mean by when you said 'Yes black people who weren't born here should go back to their country they were born in'. Is that what you were saying?

J: Well it's just the ones I don't get on with. I think that if they don't get on with everybody, that if they were born somewhere else, if they wanted to come over here that they have got to try and and get on and not be nasty to people they've just come to meet.

Int: White people you mean?

J: Yes. And some of them, the ones I don't like, they're just nasty and think that they own the country. Like the white people think that no-one owns it and they let the people come in and then they just cheat them and they can come in whenever they want.

Int: Who are you thinking of when you say this? Are you thinking of children at this school or people outside?

J: People outside mainly because you're walking down the street and you see a black person and they just start, if they're older and thin and they're perfect, and they see somebody fat coming down the street they call them 'Fatty'.

Int: Does that happen to you?

J: Yes.

Int: And what did you think?

J: I thought like saying 'Why don't you go back to where you come from?'.

Int: Was this a boy or a girl or a man or a woman who said it?

J: Well it's usually teenagers. It's usually boys and girls.

Int: Is it usually Asian or West Indian or both?

J: Both. No, I don't think black people call it so much, but the brown they call it me quite a lot.

How should we interpret this? There are a number of pieces of experience that she brings together here. One is her experiences of finding some children difficult to get on with. This is confirmed by Nina's remark that 'none of us get on well with her'. Some of the children she can't get on with are black – but not all black children: some like Gurjit are 'mardy', others like Jasmine are 'fun'. She justifies blaming those black children who are mardy in terms borrowed from a commonplace racist formulation: they have an obligation to be nice to white people because it isn't their country. (She acknowledges that black people who are born here don't fit her argument, without resolving that contradiction.) She finds additional support for her case in her experiences of being called 'Fatty' (an issue on which she is particularly sensitive) by black people in the street: this is evidence for her that they 'think they own the country'.

Our discussions with Jacky demonstrate how common-sense racist ideas achieve their power by their ability to provide convincing explanations of real problems. They also illustrate Robert Miles's remark about racism that 'it should always be remembered that

colour'. I don't really know because I've never been like
that. I don't see why you should be racist because I've got a
really good friend who is black. I mean they've done nothing
wrong, so why should we do it to them?

The same issue emerged during a discussion we had, also at
Woodshire school, with two black boys and two white girls, Amjad,
Imran, Gemma and Tina. Imran said

They say 'Go back to your own country. Go back to Paki land' and
all this. They say 'You're taking over the whole world'. Because
there are more Indians in Birmingham.

Gemma responded by placing this experience at the interpersonal
level into a wider political context, and inverting the argument.

G: It's like I was saying earlier the white people are taking over
     the world from the black people because there was a white
     president, I think it was, and he made a rule that white
     people come first and black people can have second best.

Int: But something Tina said, she said 'Some white people say
     that all these black people come over here and there isn't
     enough room'.

T: That's what the white people say, they say it makes the
     country untidy because they want all the white people in
     this country and they think the black people should be in
     theirs, but in India there is white people in India, but the
     black people aren't bothered. My cousin has gone over to
     India and he's white and they're not bothered if there's
     white people but when black people come over here the
     white people . . .

G: When the black people go over to our country we treat them
     like dirt, but when we go over to their country they treat us
     really nice and they respect us. They say 'Would you like
     this, would you like that?'.

Int: How do you know?

G: Because I've been abroad quite a few times and every time
     we go abroad they are always nice to me. They say 'Hello'
     and 'Thank you'.

I: It's because you're different like. That's why they like you.

G: Yes, they respect you. If they come over to our country they will most probably expect us to treat them the same way, but we don't.

T: Sometimes we should have some black people in our country with white people, and some white people over the black countries so that the black people can kind of make friends with the white people, and then they can come over when they want and it's the same as the white people going over to the black people's country.

The discussion continued to move between the general political level and their own specific experiences, using the one to reinforce the other. Gemma and Tina took the principle that ideally underlay their interpersonal relationships, equality of treatment, and applied it in a very concrete way to issues at the societal level.

Karen

In these discussions Gemma, Jane and Tina were drawing on ideas about racial equality that they had worked out before we spoke to them. A discussion we had with Karen at Greenshire school is particularly interesting because it reveals her in the process of working out her ideas as we talked. This was our second discussion but the first time that we had mentioned 'race'. We were talking about people arguing and we asked if sometimes black people and white people argued. Karen's response was to reflect on an act of racial discrimination by her friend Lorna's father, and to come to the realisation that she had colluded in Lorna's racism. The disjointed syntax indicates that these are ideas in the process of formation as she speaks.

K: I think at one point Lorna's dad, I don't think he likes Blacks – I don't know – but Lorna never has no Blacks to her birthday or anything. Because of that Lorna you know she's like – if her dad don't like them she won't – well actually she hangs around with – I don't know, but she couldn't invite those to her birthday party. But that ain't right because she invited – well that was yonks ago in the first year of this school. But she said to me that if you invite any like Mandeep or Sandeep I won't come to your birthday. Now I was stupid then because I used to be all over Lorna and if anything she said I would do it, because I did this.

Int: Why do you think that was stupid?

K: Because you shouldn't say that. Blacks are just the same as other people. And anyway – is that blackmail – kind of blackmail isn't it? And anyway because they're black, they're only a different colour. I've always got along with black people. Sir, do you know why some people hate Blacks, because now I'm getting a funny feeling in my tummy and it's getting mad why people hate them. It's getting mad like people kill people. I can't understand that. Some people do though. Do you know why some people hate Blacks?

Int: I was going to ask you the same question.

K: I don't know why.

During our discussion she kept worrying away at her own concerns. She switched her thinking to colonialism and then South Africa. She said that 'some white countries want to rule over black countries' and we asked her where she had got that idea from.

K: I think I've heard about that, I don't know. Some white countries did used to rule over black countries didn't they. Where Nelson Mandela lives. And he was put in jail. That was very very wrong that was, badly wrong. Whoever did that should be put in jail themselves.

Int: Why was he put in jail do you know?

K: He fought for his country or something, and I don't know, something like that. What does 'fought for his country' mean? It means like some people had just let it go and just think 'Oh well if they're going to kill us or something, we'd better back off', but he wouldn't do that. He would keep on. That's right and I want to know why do – I know God must have made them like this – but why do they have to be prejudiced against – I know you wouldn't like it, but why is it black people that people hate? Not everybody hates but why is it black people?

She then began to talk about racist name-calling at school.

K: Ah some people at this school call you 'Chocolate Face' or 'Bobble Head' if you have a bobble on your head or a black face but they don't do that because – it's just a thing to get you angry. It is, and you get dead upset about that don't you? But some people just say it to get them dead angry, they don't realise what they are saying.

Int: How do you know that they don't really hate black people?

K: Some people might. If you think about it, the black people have white best friends. Like Nicola, her gang they're all white apart from Dian and Bhupinder, you see.

Her train of thought then switched back to South Africa.

K: What person was it who put Nelson Mandela in jail and why did he?

Int: Well it was the government in South Africa which is all white people.

K: All white people. Now some black people would think 'Them white people have put Nelson Mandela in jail' and now they hate white people because white people put – you see that's . . .

Int: How do you know that some black people think that? I was wondering why you say it?

K: But it could start like that couldn't it? Anyway why can't black people rule their own country? Is it because of the government?

Int: Well in South Africa most of the people are black but there are some white people there and they run the government.

K: [Sarcastically]. They've got to run the government. Have they got to run it because they are white?

Int: Well they said that only the white people can make the laws and the black people have got to do . . .

K: Oh I wish you hadn't told me that. Oh, it's horrible that is, isn't it? Yes I suppose I have talked – my dad I've just remembered. Sort of like you go on to other things don't you when you've been talking, but that is a dreadful thing to say that is, just because they're a different colour.

Karen said that she hadn't had any lessons about these issues at school. We asked her if she thought that black people always get treated fairly in this country. Her answer illustrates again the characteristic movement of thought between personal experience and understandings about issues at the level of society, as ideas at each level are brought to bear to illuminate the other.

> It depends. Sometimes I bet some people, like if a black person did something wrong, they would say 'I know about you type of people', because of their colour. I think – we went swimming with the school once and our swimming teacher said something about that – 'I know about you type of people'. I think she did, I can't remember, because these black people were in the swimming pool and they weren't watching where they were going and people were trying to have a swim and she could have said 'Could you just go down there please' instead of saying that.

This discussion with Karen illustrates how children can develop racially egalitarian ideas largely by themselves, and how personal experiences, in Karen's case very perceptively grasped, play a central role in children's understanding of 'race'.

Charlotte

The ways in which ideas about 'race' relate to various aspects of children's lives, sometimes in problematic ways, were brought out in our discussions with Charlotte at Hillside school. We asked her if she thought that black and white people were treated the same in society. Her immediate response was to draw a parallel with the Irish situation.

> It's like, I wish we could all just live together. It's like the bombing, those Irish people who were put in jail just because they are Irish they just connected them with the IRA, they were made to say it because they kept battering them so they were made to say it.

We asked her if she thought the same was true for black people.

C: Yes, that's what happens to them, especially Jamaicans.

Int: What sort of things happen?

C: Say if there is a white person or a black person who did a robbery or something, the black person would get the worst treatment. He would just be treated like if your hand touched dung.

We asked her how she knew. She said 'I've seen in town. People calling black people . . .'. Another source of information for her was television.

Every time I've seen the news I've heard that most people who are in [prison] for life are black. Most people who are black are in for life. It makes you sick really, because I've seen people that have done worst things than that and they're out, on the news, like attacked someone and killed them, they're out, but if that person is black he would have been in for life. I don't think that is right, it's not fair.

She went on to say

C: I think grown-ups think they have a right to beat Jamaicans in. Think they've got the right to control the Jamaicans' life.

Int: Why do you think some white people think like this?

C: I reckon they're jealous. Jealous because they are getting all the attention, so if they make a fight in front of the public they will probably be in the papers. They will get more attention.

Int: What sort of attention do black people get that they are jealous of?

C: Subject in parliament . . . Grown-ups think that's not fair because they don't really belong to this country, why should they have their name in parliament and we don't. That's what they think – jealous.

She also said that people say 'Go back to your own country'. We asked her what they meant.

C: They mean 'Go back where you belong', 'Go back to your own home', 'We don't want you here', but the only reason they have come over here is because they haven't got enough money and they've got jobs over here.

Int: Do you think that people should be able to go wherever they like to get jobs?

C: Yes. Because most taxi drivers are Asian or Jamaican. That's only because no-one else would let them have a job.

The idea of discrimination immediately evoked a personal experience of discrimination.

Because my mum is selling the house, there's some Pakistani people coming round and mum says to me 'If that's a Pakistani, if a Pakistani comes, just tell him I'm not in'. I'm not to let anyone in because she don't want to really sell the house to them. I don't know why.

She contrasted the experience of discrimination faced by black people in Britain with that of British people abroad, again drawing on personal experience and on television.

C: My uncle he went to live in Spain for a bit and he never got treated bad. So why should we treat them bad? I don't know what his name was but he wrote a letter to Maggie [i.e. the then Prime Minister] and he said 'We wouldn't treat you like that so why don't you let us keep in this country? We've got no money, we've got no jobs, that satisfies you don't it Maggie? That really satisfies you if we've got nothing'.

Int: Someone wrote that did they?

C: Yes, it was on the news a couple of months ago, around Christmas.

We asked her about black people who had been born in Britain.

C: They're British then aren't they, because if they were born in this country they're British. This is their home, like Rafaqat he was born in this country, this is his home. Pakistan isn't his home, it's here. Because he was born here, as far as we're concerned he's white because he was born here. He's British.

Charlotte had a perceptive understanding of racism on television. She described an incident in a comedy programme where there was a joke at the expense of Pakistani people, 'and everyone laughed at it but I just couldn't'.

Int: Because it was a joke making fun of black people?

C: Mm, and the boy was really horrible the way he put it. There's some game-shows I've seen where they've never, ever had a Pakistani or Jamaican bloke in it. They just wouldn't.

Int: Why not?

C: I don't know. I saw *Points of View* and I saw on that once this Jamaican woman wrote and said why didn't games have Jamaican or Pakistani people on their programme.

Int: What about a programme like *Blind Date*? Could there be a black person on that?

C: Yes, there was once. And when the man picked the black lady who was No. 3, his face dropped. He tried to smile but he couldn't. He didn't even kiss her. It was horrible really because he just held her as far away as possible. It was like she was an alien – green with two horns coming out. Just think what she must have felt. I mean everyone else kissing them and when she came on he just held her shoulders.

What help had Charlotte had in developing these ideas? As the reference to her mother selling the house indicates, her mother didn't share her views. Charlotte told us that her parents believed the Irish prisoners were guilty, and her mother refused to give any money to the school's Ethiopian appeal: 'Money should go to our country, not them over there'. Charlotte avoided discussions with them.

I don't talk about it with my mum because she always says 'You're not old enough, don't worry about it'. My dad thinks that black people should up and leave to their own country. I don't talk about it – I daren't because I get into a mardy and then I get told off.

Nor had she had discussions about these issues in lessons at school. There seemed to be two influences on her thinking. One was her baby-sitter, an older girl, with whom she often talked about such issues. The other was her personal experience, not so much of black friends at school (there was only one black girl in her class and she wasn't in Charlotte's group of friends) but in her family.

I used to hate them, but they're really nice people, because my cousin Rachel she's got a boyfriend who is Jamaican – he's just got his first single out – and he's really nice and the people my cousin went round with they were really nice. But I used to hate them.

Charlotte thought that anti-racist teaching would be a good idea, couching her answer characteristically in terms of developing reciprocity of feelings, the feelings that she herself evidently had so strongly.

If they knew how Asian children and Jamaican children felt, if an Asian child and a Jamaican child were allowed to stand up and tell them how they felt, how people call them names like 'Blackie' and things like that, I think they would stop it.

We were very interested to know how her friends in the groups of girls saw these issues.

C: I don't tell anyone.

Int: Why not?

C: People might . . . I've heard it on telly calling them 'Paki-lover' and everything like that.

Int: Might they? So why does it worry you being called 'Paki-lover'?

C: Because they might not be my friends.

Int: Is that because they don't like black people?

C: No. [i.e. No they don't.]

Int: How do you know they don't like them?

C: Because in the playground they just talk like 'Pakis' [said contemptuously] as though they're a piece of dirt, it's really horrible.

Int: Do you ever say anything or do you keep quiet?

C: Keep quiet.

Charlotte doesn't share her ideas with her friends because, echoing the remarks earlier of Stuart and Tricia at the same school, she suspects they might call her a 'Paki-lover'. This fear is a powerful censor because of the way in which it could be used against her as a weapon in the war of 'negative gossip' that regulates their friendship relations. It is an example of how racism is taken up, animated and amplified by peer group social processes. This is the dilemma she is caught in.

Sometimes I can't always understand myself because I tell someone but then it's my own fault because instead of telling them I just shut up. I don't know why. Say I tell Sarah and then Sarah tells Vicky, and Vicky will tell . . . and then it will go all round the school.

Charlotte explained that she thought that her friends had racist views. 'They think Pakistani people are different, they're not human beings, just because they're black.' But they didn't make racist remarks to black children, for two reasons. One was that they didn't want to get into trouble. The other was that they treated black children in the class as exceptions. Charlotte found this contradiction difficult to understand.

C: I don't really understand it because they are always talking about 'Pakis' but the next minute they're playing with Zabeel and Ghazala and Kevin. It's very confusing. One minute they don't like them and the next minute they are playing with them.

Int: Are you saying that sometimes they don't like Kevin or Zabeel, or are you saying that they always like them and when they talk about West Indians or 'Pakis' they are thinking about other people?

C: Yes, they're thinking about other people. They think that about 'Pakis' but they think that Zabeel is like us, that Zabeel's white and they treat him as though he's white.

Chapter 7

Sources of racism

We are going to look now at some of the most important influences on white children's ideas about 'race'. The 'official' culture of the school is obviously one, and we shall deal with that in the next chapter. In addition to the school, the most important sources are parents, the community, and television.

PARENTS

It is a common idea among teachers that children who make racist remarks are simply imitating their parents (or other adults in their families). While it is true that the racist views of some children do parallel those of their parents, it would be wrong to see this as a simple process of reflection. We need to emphasise how children refashion ideas about 'race' for their own purposes. This may entail rejecting the racist views of their parents, or conversely engaging in racist behaviour which their parents strongly disapprove of. It is also worth noting that children often have adults in their family who offer a variety of different models in terms of views about 'race'. And even when children do echo the views of adults in their family, they have to try out these ideas and see if they 'work' in the context of children's culture.

Here is an example of a boy at Woodshire school 'trying out' the views of his grandmother in discussion, with which, from the evidence of the text and of other remarks that James made to us elsewhere, it is fair to assume that he has some sympathy. Trying them out entails making them stand up against the anti-racist views of two girls, Emma and Carla. The function of his disclaimers of racist views, the device of presenting them as the views of his grandmother, is to protect himself from any personal criticism while he sees how well the ideas 'work' in debate.

J: I don't know, she just thinks there's too many blacks in England and there are already a few in Parliament and she thinks in a couple of years' time they will probably be ruling England and she doesn't want them to. She thinks that they should just go back to their own country.

E: I don't think they should. We should have a mix of people.

J: I like black people.

E: So do I, especially Nina – they're dead nice to me. Sort of like my second-best friend.

J: She doesn't mind the British Blacks, they're all right, but Blacks that are Indian . . .
   [. . .]

J: My nan thinks that everyone in our school, well a few of my friends are always getting bullied by Blacks and it's true that the Blacks are always bullies, near enough.

Int: Would you agree with that?

C: There's more white bullies than black bullies I would reckon.

E: I don't think so.

J: There's more Blacks.

In an earlier discussion James had shown some insight into the fact that his grandmother had had to come to terms with important historical changes in British society which she might have found difficult to accept. We had asked James if she thought the presence of black people in Britain was a problem.

J: Yes. My nan says it is because she says it will be ruining England. They will take over England soon my nan says and you know they'll get to be prime ministers soon because they're in the government now aren't they some of them. . . . I'm not against them myself.

Int: So why does your nan feel worried about there might be a black prime minister?

J: You know when our nan was about our age, there was hardly any Blacks here and they were treated as slaves really weren't they? Like to her it seems a bit weird that they've suddenly gone into politics and things.

However, as we have seen already with Charlotte, children did not necessarily accept the racist views of their parents. This is Jane, a girl at Woodshire school.

J: My dad is a bit racist you see, he doesn't like black people. He says 'Go back to your own country' and things like that and I don't like that because I've got a lot of good friends. I've got some best friends who are coloured and they're nice. They're just the same as us.

Int: Why do you think your father feels like that and you feel differently?

J: I don't know. There was a black person on *The Krypton Factor* last night and he says 'Oh she's got no chance'. He just doesn't like black people.

Int: Why did he say that do you think?

J: He often says they shouldn't come over to our country, they're spoiling our country and things like that. Because there are a lot of people in our country and he says they're crowding up our country and things like they do in their country.

Int: But you don't think that?

J: No.

Int: And you say you think differently because you've got a lot of black friends.

J: Yes, but black people are just the same as us really. They don't do any harm to us really. It's not their fault that they're brown, it's how they were born. They need the brown to give them protection. I don't really see why you should call them 'Blackbird' and things like that.

Int: There must be quite a lot of parents who think the same way as your father.

J: Probably, yes.

It is interesting that when we suggested that she had anti-racist views because she had black friends, she responded with a general statement of equality that went beyond personal relationships. In a later discussion she made the distinction explicit.

Int: Do you think there are some people, older children or grown ups, that really don't like black people?

J: I think it is adults mostly. My dad is a bit racist. It's funny actually. He was saying 'Go back to your own country' and everything and I said 'Don't you talk like that to my friends' and he said 'How many black friends have you got' and I told him, and he said 'Well I've got much more than that', so I said 'Why do you say "Blackie" and everything?' and he says 'Because they are crowding up our country'.

Int: Does that mean that you can have a few black friends and like them, really like them, but still think that there are too many black people here and that they should go away?

J: Yes.

Some children's parents had clearly anti-racist views, which were shared by their children. Gemma, for instance, told us 'my mum doesn't believe in treating different people if they're English, between Catholics and Germans and Indian people, she thinks it's not fair'. A number of children gave us accounts of incidents when they had used racist name-calling in spite of the views of their parents and got into trouble as a result. This is Gillian at Greenshire school.

Once when I was about two years younger we used to have this coloured paper boy and I used to hate his guts. He used to call me 'slut', so once it just came out, I just said 'Fuck off you Black back to where you come from' because he used to say stuff to me and everything like 'I should belong in the ice-cream van where I come from'. That just came out and I got grounded for a month.

Her mother stopped her from going out to play for a month. We asked Gillian why she thought her mother had acted like this.

Because I called him a Black. Make him go back to where he came from, and I'd never usually swore before and that's why I got done. Because my mum doesn't like me to say anything about someone's colour.

Finally, we would draw attention to one important factor affecting parental influence. A number of the parents of the white children had friends or workmates who were black. This seemed to be particularly the case at Greenshire school, perhaps because it was in a new housing estate, where relationships were more likely to be made, perhaps because the social composition of the estate was younger and more 'upwardly mobile' than the more traditional working-class areas of the other two schools. Perhaps it was also significant that there was a higher proportion of Sikhs as against Muslims, compared with the neighbourhoods of the other two schools. Whatever the combination of causes, the result was a growing network of inter-ethnic relationships among white and Asian adults. Significantly, it was the women who were most responsible for them. Sometimes it was through work, as in the case of Kirsty's mum: 'My mum doesn't see anything wrong with different coloured people. Her best friend at work is Indian. I think that's probably why'. Sometimes it was as neighbours, brought together especially by the common experiences and problems of child-care, as we saw with Robert and Jagdeep's mothers. The emergence of these friendship-relations provided a new and inhospitable context for racialised forms of interaction among children.

TELEVISION

Television was one of the white children's most important sources of information, ideas and values about issues of 'race' (Gunter and McAleer, 1990). Most of the coverage of 'race' that they referred to involved violence and fighting, usually black against white, whether in a foreign or British context. This material could be interpreted by children in two different ways, to help construct and reinforce racist, or anti-racist, understandings.

Many children were aware of the existence of racist attacks on black people through television. In some cases they had seen it on the news. This is Adam at Greenshire school.

> You hear on the news about this alarm system in an Asian house. They'd been throwing bricks and stuff through the windows with notes on them on saying 'You will die on a certain day' and they just pressed the button and the police came round straight away. Some white people had gone out in groups and were just throwing bricks and stuff through people's windows and letter bombs through their letter-boxes and things like that.

Some children also made reference to drama programmes, *The Bill* and *Grange Hill* were two commonly mentioned, Tricia recognised the intended anti-racist message.

Do you watch *Children's Ward?* There was a gang of white boys and they were beating a different coloured lad up, and you saw them calling him names and smacking him and thumping him and they got a knife and cut him and he had to go to hospital, and you saw him in hospital then. All the people in the ward were calling him names and stuff because he was a different colour. Sometimes there's programmes like that where white children beat coloured children up.

She also talked about *Grange Hill.*

The girls are white and there's a different coloured girl that is black and all these white boys were calling her names and picking on her because she was the only one in their form, and the girls started calling the boys names and telling them to shut up.

We asked her why she thought they showed that on *Grange Hill.*

I think on *Grange Hill* sometimes they show things like drugs and stuff, not to take them, because they show you what happens when you take them. There's a song *Grange Hill* made about drugs and they just show you things not to do. I think they were trying to show you not to beat them up because they are just the same as us but a different colour.

But it was also possible to interpret the television coverage of 'race' in ways that reinforced alleged characteristics and habits of black people, especially a disposition to violence, as in the following discussion with James, Emma and Carla. This is another example of children working out their position in discussion. One theme of the discussion, as of others we have quoted, is the relationship between particular personal experiences and generalised statements about society. It is also noteworthy that it is James, who is criticised by the girls for having racist views, who poses the question of racist bias in news coverage.

E: Most of the time people that break into places, most of them are Blacks, well lots of them are Whites as well, but Blacks do it as well.

Int: More Blacks? How do you know that?

E: Because like on the news, you see black people all the time.

J: Like with the guns and everything and throwing stones.

Int: Where's that, with the guns and throwing stones?

C: Ireland.

E: Not Ireland.

J: They chuck stones through the pub windows when they have had a few drinks. You hear it on the news that a few Blacks got drunk in the pub and they got chucked out for a little bit of violence and they got rough outside and started chucking bricks through the windows.

E: Some black people are lovely – I don't mean sexy. I like Lenny Henry.

We asked if they were saying that more black people do this than white people.

J: Yes. Well it might not be, because most of the reporters for the news are white and they might not want to show you Whites.

Int: Do you think that might be true?

C: No. They have to do a good job don't they, so they have to do what people say.

J: Yes, but it might be, you don't know.

Int: So you think that it doesn't matter whether the reporters are black or white, they just tell what is the truth?

E: Yes, they do.

C: You're just against Blacks.

J: No, I'm not.

C: You are.

J: No I'm not. Shut up, this is about friends this is, not arguing.

Int: Why do you say that James is against black people?

E: Because he says black people do this wrong and black people do that.

J: Some do.

E: Yes, some of them, but not all black people are horrible.

J: I'm not saying all of them do.

E: Yes, but you're sort of talking about Blacks all the time.

J: So are you.

E: No I'm not.

Int: But James said that more black people are bullies and more black people are violent.

J: Yes, that's what I think, because Amjad is always beating me.

C: Probably in this school, yes.

J: I reckon there's more white bullies in this school than black, like Lee.

Some children did comment on racist bias in television. Without prompting, Ben, a white boy at Woodshire school (the same boy who makes some racist remarks about Asian shops later in this chapter), made this perceptive comment about the programme *Till Death Us Do Part* (contrary to the BBC's protestations about the programme (BBC, 1973).

B: Like the programme called 'Alf Garnett', that's doing no good because there's a white man in that and he's bald and there's a black man in it that lives with him and that isn't doing very good because he encourages him to say that like 'black something' and 'black' this and 'black' that. 'I don't want to live with a Blackie' and things like that.

Int: And you think that people get encouraged to say that when they see people saying it on the telly?

B: Yes.

It was the opinion of Kevin, a black boy at Hillside school, that any portrayal of racist behaviour on the television tended to encourage it, even if the intent was the opposite. We were talking about his experiences of racist name-calling.

Int: But where do these ideas come from?

K: Well on telly last night I seen these white people calling these black people 'black bastards'.

Int: On the telly? What programme was that?

K: *The Bill*. They should stop it.

Int: What, they should stop saying things like that on the telly?

K: Yes, because it's only getting other people to say it to any West Indian boy. And then they would stop saying it.

Most media researchers would agree with Charles Husband that 'What you see depends on where you are standing and what you are looking for' (Husband, 1975, p. 34). Kevin recognised that the depiction of racism on television, because it resonates with populist and stereotypical views of Blacks in Britain, has the potential to reinforce and legitimate racist ideas, invoking sympathy and support from at least some members of the TV audience.

Television is also a powerful source of ideas about black people in the Third World. We want to quote again from the discussion we had with James, Emma and Carla, because it illustrates how many children make use of disparate images and ideas picked up from television in order to construct a theory of Britain and the Third World. We take up the discussion where they have been talking about the views of people in their families that 'black people are taking over'.

E: My nan and grandad don't really mind as long as they don't take over our country because we're not taking over their country are we? We're not going over there with all men like and hunting for animals and everything, well some people are, like tigers and elephants. Black people look nice on the telly . . .

J: Yes because their teeth look dead white and ours don't.

E: And they ride on the elephants and there was a little box thing . . .

J: And they strap it under the elephant and then they sit in it.

E: And they put white people in it, but it's not many black people is it, it's only the black people riding the elephant and then it's the white people in the box, in the shade.

Int: Why is that?

J: Because the Blacks in Africa and that think the white people are so great, they think they're brilliant because they've got all this water and food and these dead good clothes and that.

C: Yes like in *Indiana Jones and the Last Crusade*.

E: I think it was Princess Diana wasn't it sitting in the back once? Yes, that's it and they were all greeting them and everything and they took them to this dead nice . . .

J: They were just going like that to touch the elephant. They thought the elephant was good as well because of Princess Diana. They think Whites are brilliant but a white princess . . .

E: They play music and drums for them when they come and greet them and they have a party.

We asked if black people everywhere thought that Princess Diana was wonderful.

E: No, I don't think so.

J: Well most of them do.

E: Some people are probably jealous of Princess Diana.

J: She's dead pretty, that's why.

E: She's gots lots of clothes, she goes to places like Australia, she lives in a posh house. They're probably jealous because they just wear little rags round them.

They continued reproducing stereotyped images of Africa: hunting, catching fish, washing their clothes in the river, worshipping their gods, dressing up in war paint. We asked them how they knew this and they said they had seen it on television: Tarzan.

The images of the Third World constructed by these children on the basis of television and film representations demonstrate in graphic terms how the media continue to project limited and distorted pictures of these countries. The information we receive about the Third World is rarely good news, unless it is made so by the intervention of white people: a royal visit, a powerful saviour (Indiana Jones, Tarzan), charity for the famine-ridden. The heavy consumption of television by children and its centrality in conversations with friends and the family serves to underline the point that media-derived images are likely to exert a profound and lasting impression on how they see and interpret what life is like outside Britain. Ghazala was aware of the dangers of television presenting negative sterotypes of non-Western countries from her own experience of visiting Pakistan. She had brought into school photos of her visit which contrasted with the images presented by a television programme the class had watched.

G: In the programme they're making it look like as if there's lots of beggars and, if they're going to bed, throwing so many clothes on the floor, things like that, and it's not like that. . . . It's not dirty like that.

Int: Do you think that children in the class, the white children, think that Pakistan is all dirty and all like that?

G: Some don't and some do. Because Dawn said 'Is Pakistan like that?' and I go 'No' and she goes 'I thought it weren't' because when I brought the photos in the place looked all clean.

Int: What about children who watch that programme, white children, and who don't have a chance to see your photos, perhaps children in another school, what do you think they would think?

G: Probably just think it's all messy and they would never like to go there for a trip or a holiday and they don't know how they live there.

Given the partial and often ethnocentric orientation of media coverage of the Third World it is not surprising to find that White children's images are structured along similar lines.

SHOPS

In *Racism and the Mass Media* (1974) Paul Hartmann and Charles Husband distinguish two sources of information about 'race', media sources and situational sources, and stress the importance of situational factors in creating racial hostility; 'heavy consumption of mass media does not in itself lead to greater or less hostility towards coloured people. Hostility seems to be much more a situationally generated characteristic' (Hartmann and Husband, 1974, p. 109). The situations that they investigate are in the neighbourhood, the locality, the community. We want to widen our focus from the school as a key institution in the community to look at children's interpretations of 'race' in relation to local Asian shops.

Local Asian-run shops are an important social site in terms of 'race'. They are perhaps the only institution where white children and adults regularly interact with black adults. They may be, and often are, an object of racist behaviour (Ekblom *et al.*, 1988). They are certainly a symbol of social change. The customer–shopkeeper relationship, with its attendant potential for tensions and conflicts, is one that may be easily racialised. As such, the Asian local shop as a social site may be a source or confirmation of racialised 'social representations' circulating within the local white community. We shall, however, bear in mind Hartmann and Husband's proposition that the hostile responses of white people to black people moving into an area can have various causes, not just that of racial prejudice (Hartmann and Husband, 1974, pp. 91–2).

In the following extract we see three boys from Woodshire school – Ben, Richard and Simon – trying to make sense of their personal experiences in the context of the common-sense knowledge of the community and in terms of their own attitudes to 'race'.

B:　Most of the places round here are corner shops and off-licences are mostly run by black people. Because there are places called Evans, it was named after this white pair called Mr and Mrs Evans and they still haven't changed it.

R:　And then when they moved these black people moved in and I said to my dad 'What do you think they will call it now?' and he said jokingly 'Probably Mr and Mrs Poppadoms.'

S:　There's a joke like that – 'Why did the Roman builders build straight roads? So that Pakis couldn't go in corner shops.'

B:　And the only place round here where I know off that has got white people in it is the Post Office up Grantley Road and they still go up there and they still go by quarters in sweets and ounces.

S:　That's going to get sold though but it's still going to be run by white people.

B:　In the black shops their hands are always filthy and they always check your bags, they always tip your bags out.

S:　But next door where they give you quarters, their hands are always clean and they've always got a sink in the main piece and they wash their hands every time they do quarters. And say you've got two and a half sweets over what you should

have they won't exactly say 'Oh you're two and a half sweets over I'll take them out'. Like the black people, they make sure you've got exactly what you paid for.
[. . .]

S: I think that happens like when we call black people some name, maybe as children they have been called this name, as we were talking about the shops and being a bit scroogy, and maybe the people in the shop have grown up with white people calling them names and they've got to not exactly like white people. Maybe that's part of the problem.

Int: And you think that might make them . . .

S: Yes, a bit agitated. Maybe they like them as customers but they wouldn't give them any more than what they deserve.

The contrast of the white and the black shops epitomises a change in the composition of the local community and changes in social relationships within it. The relationship between white shopkeepers and White customers is personal as well as strictly commercial. Simon is aware that their account lends itself to a racist reading and suggests an explanation that explains the black shopkeepers' behaviour as the product of their experience of racism. The discussion continued.

B: My dad asked to do a job there and he looked at the price and they said 'No I want it cheaper than that – it's only to put some tiles up' but tiles are quite hard to put up. My dad would buy all the stuff but they wouldn't give him the money. Every time we go in there I says, because they've got a little girl there, and my dad goes up and pays every Friday but they won't let us have the bill any more. Like Evans, I went in and asked for some toothpaste. I lost about 2p and said 'Can I put it on the bill?' and he goes 'No' so I had to run all the way back home just for 2p.

Int: Is that in Evans? So they wouldn't let you have the 2p?

S: Yes, but that was when the black people had taken over it. The white people in there would have let you off.

B: Because sometimes my mum had deliveries because when they were there my mum was having my sister and they were giving her free deliveries, because she was having a baby and it's quite far to walk.

R: When I told you about that shop that changed it to 'Paki', well this whole gang of white hooligans came in and they said 'Oi can we have some toothpaste' and he said 'Yes here's the toothpaste' and he said 'Well perhaps you could do yourself up with it'. That's what one of the hooligans said to the black person.

S: It was like I was in Evans once and there was this black lady walked in, probably one of the friends of the people, and she didn't have quite enough money and because she was black they goes 'Oh bring it in tomorrow' and there's this white lady she comes up about two customers next and she got a bit of money left over and she goes 'Can I bring it tomorrow morning?' and they goes 'No, can I have it now please'.

Int: Did you see this?

S: I saw it because I was in the queue at the time.

Int: Maybe they knew the black person and they didn't know the white person.

S: She was a regular customer because she used to babysit me and she used to go every afternoon to buy stuff.

Int: So are you saying that black people are more likely to favour other black people than white?

All: Yes, that's true.

R: Because when I went in the Paki shop up the road – Indian shop . . .

B: People keep on calling it the Paki shop.

R: And I went in and there was this lady in there – they don't do much, like there was a little girl in there. She walks out the main door to get into the actual shop, she grabs something and puts it in this bag and she said 'How much is it Dad' and 'You can have it free' and they're getting everything free. Like once I had to pay about 4p or 5p. I went to buy some washing-up liquid and I picked it up and there was about a quarter of it left.

B: I know, they only give you half of it anyway . . .

R: Like the potatoes have all got water in. Most of them are rotten.

S: There are nice ones in the bin but they just pick the rotten ones out for you.

B: But down there at that Indian shop they do overcharge people. There's this Indian girl – this fat Indian lady, she's very slow and she's getting on a bit – and there is this little girl and she knows what everything is in the shop and she knows how much it is. She gives it you quite pleasantly and then there's this old lady who walks down dead slow as if she doesn't want to serve you and then when she gets down to the counter you tell her what it is and she says 'What?' and then you tell her again and she still says 'What?'. You have to tell her about three times and then she understands. She gets it and she says 'Anything else?' and she says 'Hurry up, we've got some more customers' and then if you say you want something else she says 'Oh' and goes and gets you it. She's not very pleasant to talk to. They do overcharge you about 5p or 6p more.

According to this account, the Asian shops treat white people badly in comparison with white shops. They won't give them credit, won't let them off small sums, won't do free deliveries in cases of need, are unfriendly when serving them, sell them inferior goods, and overcharge. From the previous extract we can add that they are dirty too. Furthermore, they discriminate against white people. Black – presumably Asian – customers do get credit, and free goods. How should we read this account? One response would be to reject it as a collection of racist stereotypes with no basis in real life, but that is to refuse it any validity as a report of first-hand experiences. Of course, it is difficult without any independent evidence to know how factually correct it is, but to us it rings quite true. That is not to deny the elements of exaggeration and distortion – the washing-up liquid, the potatoes – which contribute to the construction in this account of a typical 'social representation' of an Asian shop, and which may themselves be the product of such social representations already current in the local white community. But this is a social representation which is trying to grapple with real concerns. One is that of relationships within the community, that close-knit web of expectations and obligations, based on historical experience, that make up the common culture of this traditionally white working-class neighbourhood, including those between tradespeople and customers, in both directions in this account. The taking-over of many local small shops by Asian families has broken that web. It can of course be remade, but there are obstacles. The first is simply time: to build a new historical continuity of experience. There may also be cultural obstacles, in the sense of differences in customs of behaviour: not only language barriers, but differences in when credit is given, for example. The absence of personal relationships between the shopkeepers and the white parents may mean that white children are less inhibited about petty shoplifting. There *may* be differences in hygiene standards or poor quality goods, perhaps as a consequence of lack of capital or low profitability. And of course there is racism, as Richard recognises in his report of the toothpaste incident. The question is, do white children, in attempting to come to an understanding of the complex social reality embodied in the changing local shop, adopt a *racialised* explanation as one that seems to be the most comprehensive and unified explanation, and one that is likely to be continuously confirmed by common-sense ideas within the white community?

There are contradictory elements in the understandings of the three boys: cultural material – from jokes to interpretations of personal experiences – which can crystallise into racist ideologies, and elements of anti-racist ideologies, based on notions of social justice and supported by personal and historical experience, capable of generating contrary explanations such as Simon's suggestion that the shopkeepers' experiences of racism may account for their apparent lack of friendliness to white people.

RACISM AND ANTI-RACISM IN CULTURE

We have looked at ways in which three of the principal external sources of ideologies of 'race' impinge upon children's cultures. We want to focus now on dynamics of 'race' arising within children's cultures themselves.

There are several recent ethnographic studies that have focused on the ways that themes of racism and anti-racism may coexist within the same sub-cultural configuration, and consequently may coexist, contradictorily, in white discourse and consciousness. Of these, the studies by Roger Hewitt, Simon Jones and Les Back are of particular importance.

All three writers share a recognition of two aspects of a new situation: emergence of multi-racial youth cultures in the inner cities, and the relatively common incidence of multi-racial friendships that exist within them. Roger Hewitt speaks of:

noticing, for example, that friendship between black and white youth was extremely common and was grounded in an experience of being born and growing up through primary school in mixed working-class neighbourhoods together, occupying the same recreational spaces, experiencing closely meshed life worlds and growing into adolescence with far more friendship and other network ties than had been true of their parents' generation. Secondly, black youth had been forging a distinctive and varied set of cultural practices that seemed to construct points of paradoxical access to Whites . . .

(Hewitt, 1989, p. 2)

This new culture has given rise to what Hewitt calls 'strongly expressed, community-based anti-racist stances' (Hewitt, 1989, p. 2). Simon Jones describes how some white youth had developed ' "alternative" explanations of social and political events to the prevailing discourses', particularly of racist ideologies propagated through newspapers and television (Jones, 1988, pp. 224–5). But for Jones such explicit anti-racist perspectives were not the predominant outcome.

The most pertinent and effective repudiations of racism, rather, lay embedded in the situated interaction and forms of negotiation evolved by young people themselves. For such was the intimacy of such interaction for some, that the relevance of racial stereotypes and divisions could be mitigated in the course of everyday social exchange and experiences. . . . Declarations that 'colour doesn't matter' and 'it's what's in the heart that counts' and 'you can't judge a book by its cover' rested on the sincere belief that the question of racial difference was, or at least should have been, of no significance to personal relations between Black and White.

(Jones, 1988, pp. 225–6)

There are themes here that we find echoed in the context of children's cultures. The point we want to focus on here is that of contradictory consciousness. Shared experience, cultural orientations and cross-racial friendships did not automatically lead to anti-racism. 'It was thus entirely feasible for young Whites to maintain certain common-sense racist ideas, while continuing to associate with young Blacks and appropriate black culture' (Jones, 1988, p. 216). And again Jones speaks of:

the deeply contradictory nature of white responses about race. In struggling to resolve the contradictions that resulted from

their friendships and cultural-musical influences, young Whites
constantly had to battle not only against the weight of peer-
group pressure, but also against other, more general, ideological
influences.

(Jones, 1988, p. 219)

Jones talks specifically of 'common sense' in terms that locate him
within a Gramscian framework:

Perhaps a more contradictory interpretation of 'common sense' is
required here, one which looks at the elements of practical 'good
sense' in the white working-class consciousness of race and class.
For if this book has shown anything, it is that such consciousness
is deeply contradictory.

(Jones, 1988, p. 235)

WHERE DOES ANTI-RACIST 'GOOD SENSE' COME FROM?

One source is 'elaborated' anti-racist ideologies circulating in society
that enter the cultures of children and young people 'from outside'.
One obvious source in the school context is school policies against
racist name-calling, as we shall see in the next chapter. But we need
to explain why some children develop anti-racist stances even in
the absence of school policies, or largely independently of them,
and so we have to look at internal dynamics at work within some
sub-cultures that give rise to anti-racist stances, and provide a
purchase for elaborated ideologies of racial equality. It is this aspect
that both Jones and Hewitt stress. Hewitt refers to 'spontaneous
multiculturalism' (Hewitt, 1989, p. 8). Jones argues that 'Perhaps
the most important lesson to be drawn here for any popular anti-
racist politics is that young people are already actively involved
in producing their own anti-racist solutions, regardless of political
initiatives from above'. It is 'an implicit rebuttal of racism and
nationalism more potent than any multicultural ideology' (Jones,
1988, p. 236).

We leave aside here the question of the possible political limits to
spontaneous anti-racism. Our concern here is with the sources, lying
within the cultures of young white people, of anti-racist dynamics.

Hewitt identifies two related sources: the adoption of black cultural
forms, and social interaction with black people. His research
describes the impact of black youth culture on young Whites:
clothes, music, linguistic forms, styles of behaviour. The fact of

adoption itself was both an acknowledgement and a reinforcement of the high social status of these forms. These black cultural forms were 'charged with social and political meanings', and for Hewitt it is primarily here 'away from the realm of explicit social "attitudes" and ideas, that young Whites may become instructed in the issues surrounding racism and black/white relations' (Hewitt, 1986, p. 96).

Jones notes the same phenomenon. He also, as do Hewitt and back, describes the creation of egalitarian relationships between black and white. Jones speaks of the shared experience of working-class life in the inner city leading to an ideology of 'community' based on 'a set of basic values of everyday life, values of cooperation, mutuality and reciprocity' (Jones, 1988, p. 212). Similarly, Back describes 'a domain within which "race" is temporarily deconstructed' (Back, 1991, p. 21). The space is created by the two processes we have noted: 'patterns of interaction and the sharing of cultural and linguistic materials'. Back argues that a 'de-racialised discourse' emerges because 'the lived relationships . . . of those who participate in multi-racial peer groups' are threatened by 'the disruptive potential of racism' (Back, 1991, p. 23).

The question is, what relevance has this explanation of white anti-racism for the situation of children of 10 and 11 years old living in predominantly white neighbourhoods and going to predominantly white primary schools?

The extent to which black culture had an impact on these children was very limited, for two reasons. First, these children were only beginning to enter into teenage youth culture, and any impact it might have still lay largely in the future. Second the schools were in areas where the black population was largely Asian, with few Afro-Caribbeans. The direct transmission of Afro-Caribbean culture (which is by far the most important source of cultural forms adopted by young white people) into the locality was therefore very attenuated. The penetration of black cultural elements was limited largely to the influence of mainstream commercial culture: in particular, black pop stars. Some of these were popular with the children, and conveyed a certain charge of social meaning, at least in the sense that some children saw Michael Jackson as representing a different, and preferable, image to those of white stars like Bros, Kylie Minogue and Jason Donovan.

In short, the cultural (in this sense) terrain on which these children met, played together, and established social relationships, was largely white-based. The influence of black culture could not be more than a subsidiary source of anti-racist elements among the culture of these white children.

It is therefore to processes of interpersonal interaction that we must look for the roots of white anti-racism. At this point it is necessary to step back from the specific issue of racism and look more generally at children's culture and interaction.

In an unequal society, full of competitiveness and aggression and oppressions of gender, class and 'race' it is not difficult to see how social processes of domination pervade the cultures of children, whether or not they are reinforced by the institutional culture of the school itself. But what about processes of equality, where do they come from?

We want to place our answer to this in the context of our earlier discussion of ideology. We suggested that there were two sources of critical understandings. One was elements of 'elaborated ideologies' that challenged dominant ideas and values. The other arose from people's everyday experience, which gave rise to contradictory common-sense understandings, capable of confirming but also of challenging dominant ideologies. The question we posed, and now want to offer an answer to, is what is there in the everyday experience of children that gives rise to ideologies and social processes of equality?

THE EGALITARIAN DYNAMIC IN CHILDREN'S PEER RELATIONSHIPS

We will take as our starting-point some ideas in an early work of Piaget, not the more familiar work on stages of non-social cognitive development, but his ideas about children's *social* development in *The Moral Judgement of the Child* (1932). The argument of the book is that children's social morality arises from the structure of their social relationships. Piaget distinguished between two types of social relationships in children's lives. One was relationships with adults, which were relationships between unequals. The other was relationships with peers, i.e. children of an equal status. The two types of relationships give rise to two different types of social morality. The 'morality of constraint' is engendered in the early years within the hierarchical relationship between the child and the adult. The 'morality of cooperation', a new type of morality for the child, arises from egalitarian peer relationships. Piaget distinguishes between *heteronomous* morality based on fixed eternal rules and typical of the adult–child relationship, and *autonomous* morality based on negotiated rules generated within the peer relationship. This is how Kutnick summarises Piaget's argument:

> Collective understanding and mutuality are the bases to Piaget's further stage of moral development, the 'morality of cooperation'. Unlike the morality of constraint, the morality of cooperation can develop only amongst peers, or children of an equal status. It is in the environment of equals that children are free to explore the differences between their perceptions and understandings of rules and justice. Children come from a home/adult-dominated set of rules and modes of interaction. They quickly find that these are not an adequate background for the relationships they wish to develop amongst themselves. With their different backgrounds and understanding of rules, children who wish to play with one another must learn to adapt and negotiate. The understanding of intentionality becomes more fully developed. In the interests of those children concerned, rules become changeable or mutable to maintain play. . . . Through the strength of mutuality, the peer group becomes a viable alternative to the imposition of hierarchical constraints.
>
> (Kutnick, 1988, pp. 79–80)

Though Piaget never returned to the themes of this early work, his initial insights have provided a starting point for a large number of subsequent studies, and provoked many controversies (see Modgil *et al.*, 1983, for an overview). Before making some critical points of our own, we want to outline the contribution made by James Youniss (1980), an American social psychologist, to developing Piaget's approach. Youniss's concern is with the changes that take place as children move into and through the period of middle childhood. He suggests that the basis of peer relations among children from about 5 to 8 years is joint activity. In order to accomplish it children have to negotiate rules of interaction. The principle on which they are based is 'direct reciprocity' – that is, 'I do to you what you do to me'. However, direct reciprocity 'discourages formation of a stable interpersonal relationship' (Youniss, 1980, p. 230) because it brings children together or drives them apart according to situation. This causes problems which the child comes consciously to recognise and respond to, during the years 8–10, by developing a new sort of peer relationship. 'The most important lesson which children learn with peers is that social business can be transacted smoothly only through a joint agreement to practice reciprocity for mutual ends' (Youniss, 1980, p. 271).

This new type of relationship is based on two interrelatedly developed principles. The first is that the notions of equality and reciprocity are reconstituted not as pragmatic rules of joint activity but as explicit ideal principles of relationships, based on cooperation and equal treatment. 'The practice of free and open discussions where everyone's opinions have an equal chance to be heard leads naturally to a belief that fairness demands equality in treatment and in outcomes' (Youniss, 1980, p. 255). The second is the growth of understanding of the individual. The new peer relationship depends upon the ability to move away from an egocentric viewpoint and take the perspective of the other.

In the context of 'race', the development of these two interrelated processes was testified to by many children we spoke to, Katherine at Greenshire school explained that she had stopped using racist name-calling because she realised how much it hurt black children, even though their reverse name-calling didn't upset her.

K: I just don't say it anymore, I've just stopped saying it.
Int: When do you feel like saying it?
K: Like I can remember I was having an argument with someone who was black and they were saying things like 'You white duck' and all things like that, and at that time I felt like saying it but I didn't because I think that it would really upset them if we said it, but if they say it to us because it wouldn't really upset me.

The combination of the growth of psychological insight into the other and the development of an egalitarian social morality is the principal cause of the decline of racist behaviour during the junior school years that many children remarked on. This is Paul at Hillside school.

P: I don't do it as often, no, I used to do it when I was smaller because I thought it was funny, but I don't think it is as good now.
Int: Why not?
P: Because I've grown up a bit more now and I understand how much they get hurt, more their feelings.

These changes in social relationships provide a material basis for the development of generalised ideas of racial equality. Stuart at

Hillside school had given us an elaborated explanation of racial discrimination. We wondered where his ideas had come from.

Int: Are these things that your mum and dad have talked to you about?

S: No, I've been seeing them on programmes. I've been thinking what it would be like if I was a Black person and somebody started calling me names and making up jokes about me, and I thought it would be really horrible. So I just got it out of my mind.

According to Piaget, the child's development of the concept of social justice is as follows. Up till age 5, justice means obedience to authority – the rules laid down by parents. By age 7–8, as a result of the experience of cooperative play with peers, the child has developed a concept of justice based on equality. By age 11–12, as a result of the child's growing awareness of individual differences, the concept of equity has been developed (i.e. of equality modified to take account of difference) (Leahy, 1983). Piaget sees this as a developmental progression, parallel to that in non-social cognition (from concrete to formal operations).

Piaget has been criticised on the grounds that his stages of moral development do not meet the criteria for developmental stages that are exemplified in his work on logico-mathematical thinking. Much subsequent work has been concerned with developing a more rigorous formulation of the stages of children's moral development. Perhaps the most influential figure here is Lawrence Kohlberg (1976), who has argued that:

> moral reasoning develops directly as a function of intellectual development and that moral reasoning reflects the application of logical principles, derived from the intellectual domain, to moral problems. . . . Moral development is a self-generating process which springs from the internal logic of thought.
>
> (Emler, 1983, p. 145)

Kohlberg's theory is based on the abandonment of Piaget's fundamental proposition that moral development is derived from social relationships.

Our own criticism of Piaget is from exactly the opposite direction. We would argue that it is the theorisation of social relationships that is underdeveloped. We will begin by making some comments on how we see Piaget's types of morality.

First, Piaget's 'morality of constraint' and 'morality of cooperation' are ideal types. As Emler notes, 'relations with parents are not exclusively relations of constraint and relations with peers are never purely co-operative' (Emler, 1983, p. 148).

Second, we see the development of moral judgement not as a linear progression through stages which supersede each other, but as the developmental acquisition, primarily through social interaction, of a repertoire of social morality. That repertoire consists of a number of elements: moral principles, psychological insight, concepts of relationships, situation-evaluating procedures, interactional strategies. Within that repertoire, we do not see a hierarchical arrangement of moral principles. It is not the case that these are in a fixed hierarchy of moral progression. This is in contrast to Piaget who saw equality as 'inferior' to equity. Nor is it the case that the principle of 'equity', based on the acknowledgement of individual differences, supersedes that of 'equality'. The application of the principle of 'equity' is not necessarily always more progressive, more socially just, than that of 'equality'. The fairness and justice of the moral position that a child takes up in any particular situation is not dependent on what moral principle is applied in itself, in the abstract, but on how the situation is constructed and interpreted by the child.

We can illustrate with an example from our work on 'race'. Take immigration. For one child, giving salience to individual differences, the principle of 'equity' requires that people with black skin should not have equality of right of entry. For another, common humanity overrides any individual differences, and requires a blanket application of 'equality'. In that situation, an appeal to 'equity' can be used to justify racist discrimination. This links with Frank Reeves's analysis of political discourse, especially his identification of 'discursive racialisation' (1983). He notes how people avoid the explicit use of 'race' in their evaluations, descriptions and prescriptions and use a lexicon which none the less justifies racist discrimination in, say, immigration legislation.

Piaget's insight into the material basis of social morality in children's relationships needs to be situated within a theory of how social relationships are socially constructed. Here we want to reintroduce the concept of ideology that we have discussed earlier, and locate children's morality within it. It is ideology that tells the child, as Therborn puts it, what is good, what is right, what exists, what is possible (Therborn, 1980, p. 18). It is through ideology that the child constructs each social situation and decides what moral principles should apply. And it is because ideology, and particularly common-sense ideology, is not unitary that we need the concept of a repertoire of social morality.

The introduction of the concept of ideology leads us to put into question the idea that equality is the single fundamental principle of children's peer relationships. This is where we want to render Piaget 'more social'. Children do not necessarily confront each other as equals. On the contrary, they live in a social field structured by ideologies of gender, class, 'race', age, ability, and so on, which tend to position children unequally in relation to each other. Other ideologies speak to them of equality, and as we have argued, drawing on Piaget's insight, the most powerful among them is that deriving from, and continuously reinforced by, everyday peer interaction. It is in the ceaseless push and pull of ideologies of equality and dominance that relationships are made and remade through social interaction.

Chapter 8

Responses to racist incidents

Black children are faced with the problem of how to respond to racist harassment. One option is to try and ignore it. This is what Kevin at Hillside school did in response to name-calling that he regarded as less offensive. He made a distinction between children saying 'nigger' to him as a one-off remark and children saying it aggressively in order to harass him and cause the maximum offence.

> K: Well when he's sort of saying like 'You nigger', sort of like that I just ignore him, but when he is shouting 'Nigger, nigger' and keeps following me and saying 'Nigger' I take it personal and just go away.

> Int: What can you do about it?

> K: Well sometimes I fight him off, sometimes I tell the teacher.

The rationale for ignoring insults was to give the impression that it wasn't having the desired effect of causing hurt, so that the user would give up, as Sandeep, a girl at Greenshire school, explains.

> If you ignore them they will think that it doesn't get to you and then they won't do it, but if you sort of beat them up, they know it is getting to you and they will say it more.

But, as her friend Parminder added, the risk of 'ignoring' is that the harassment will continue, and it is difficult to hold back your anger.

> But if you stay quiet they go on and on and on. You know it but you stay quiet, but that will inside you, you know, one day you will really get mad and you'll flipping break their legs off or something. You might beat them up really a lot if you don't do it first, because they hate you and you know it and you won't tell. It's

like hate growing inside you and you're just being nice outside like them.

In some cases children could rely on the support of other children. This was often the case for younger children who had relatively institutionalised relations of protection with older children, often a sibling. Zabeel at Hillside school was often looked to for protection by other Asian children, including Rafaqat. 'If someone beats me in the school I tell Zabeel. Zabeel is the toughest in the school.'

Sometimes white friends, like Gemma at Woodshire school, would defend black children. She was talking about her friends Nina and Yvette.

> Every time they got hurt or something I always used to stick up for them because they called them 'Paki' and everything and kept on making fun of them, their colour.

The key notion in dealing with racist harassment is 'sticking up for yourself'. That requires first of all the conscious adoption of a mental approach, as Gurjit explains. We asked her if racist name-calling used to upset her a lot.

> Used to, used to cry a lot. But now I'm sticking up for myself and getting the strength.

And again:

> I'm getting my nerve now, I feel like hitting somebody, I do, then I tell them off . . . . I get very, very angry.

Gurjit found in the experiences of her mother and her aunt contrasting models of how to deal with oppression.

> Int: It's important for people to stick up for themselves is it?
>
> N: Yes. Like my mum, when she was my age everybody used to bully her and when my auntie, my mum's sister – she lives with us – nobody would pick on her because my auntie was a big bully. Everyone used to pick on my mum because she told me everything. And like my granny she was poor then and my mum used to go to this school and she wasn't allowed to go on any trips because my gran didn't have any money and my auntie she used to go on trips, trips, trips. Like she goes to work now, she wants to get to do some more courses . . . at college. It's important to stick up.

BLACK CHILDREN CALLING WHITE CHILDREN 'RACIAL' NAMES

Many children told us of the names used by black children to white children. This is Nina.

Ice-cream face. I sort of say the opposite that they say to me.

Black children wanting to call racial names back faced several problems. First, the white racist vocabulary was much richer, as many children recognised, including Rachel, a white girl at Woodshire school.

Int: What do they say back?

R: Instead of saying 'Chocolate person' say 'White chocolate person' and things like that. They don't really make up that many names because it's harder to find names that have white in them.

Second, white children knew that there was no social sanction against white skin. Nevertheless, remarks about it could be effective, because they recognised the intent behind the remarks and accepted the principle of reciprocity, as Kerry, a white girl at Woodshire, explains. She was talking about Natasha.

K: They think that she is not going to saying anything back to them because they think 'Oh she hasn't got anything to say to me'.

Int: Right, do you mean because you can say things about her colour but she won't say things about yours?

K: They think that she's not going to say anything about their colour because there's nothing wrong with their colour but Natasha thinks up something and she says 'Oh shut up Milky Bar' to them, and they think if she's going to keep on saying that to me I'm not going to say it anymore and it dies down.

The third problem concerns the issue of 'nation'. There was no reverse equivalent to the racist name-calling of 'Paki', as Nina recognised.

N: It's like if they call you 'Silly cow' you could just say something back like 'Silly cow' back. Sometimes if they call you 'Paki' you can't say anything back.

Int: Why not?

N: Because there isn't anything to say back. Like if they say
     'Go back to your own country' you can't say it back to them
     because this is their country.

Apart from calling names back, another option in response to racist
name-calling was to hit the offender. The knowledge that children
would hit in retaliation was often an effective deterrent, even by girls
against boys, as Parminder explained.

Int: You said that Ross was someone who sometimes called
      people 'Paki' and names like that.

P: Yes I know. He doesn't – well he does but that's mostly
      when he is out of school. He swears a lot when he is out
      of school as well. In school he wouldn't call it, like once or
      twice somebody 'Paki' right, but otherwise he wouldn't. He
      wouldn't call me it now. He knows that I can beat him in,
      that's why. So if he did I would smack his face in. That's
      what I do with anybody.

Int: What about outside school?

P: Still if I heard him call me 'Paki' I would still beat him
      in.

As well as deterring, hitting relieves your own feelings, and as we have
seen earlier, children can experience very strong aggressive emotions
in conflict situations. This is Nina again (and it's interesting that this
and the previous extracts are from Asian girls).

Int: So if you started hitting people back who said things like that
      would that make you not so upset?

N: Yes, probably, because you can get all the anger on to them
      and take your anger out on them.

Int: So is that the problem that when people say things like that
      your anger stays inside you because you can't get back at
      them properly?

N: Yes.

But here black children faced a dilemma. Hitting was against the
school rules. The problem with hitting is that you may get into
trouble with teachers as a result, most likely through the person you
hit telling them in order to get you into trouble. For many children
the dilemma was made more complex because of a third factor. Some

of their parents, such as Parminder's in the following extract, had advised them to respond to racist name-calling by hitting. (Miss G is the headteacher.)

> When people pick on my brother I beat them in. My dad goes to me 'Whether you to go to Miss G, if somebody says anything to you right – if somebody hits you once you hit them twice'. And my dad goes 'If they hit you twice you hit them four times'. He goes 'Double it always'. Because they won't fight again then.

The legitimacy of hitting back to defend yourself seemed to some children to be an important truth about life in the world outside school. In this discussion at Woodshire school with Tina, Imran and Amjad, they referred to a murder that had taken place a few days earlier in the locality.

I: You asked me about why you need to be strong. Well my dad has got a shop and I walk home at night. There are drunk people, hippies and all that, and they come up to you and they start saying stuff like 'Paki'. In town there is this sort of pub, with the skinheads and punks. They start being cheeky and kids walk past them and they start pushing you around, so I hit them.

T: That's why they learn to be tough because if people pick on them when they're outside, or walking home from kind of hockey, sometimes when we're playing hockey sometimes when we go home it is getting dark, and there are all youths about. They kind of pick on them and bully them.

A: Like sometimes you can die if you don't stick up for yourself. Like this man got stabbed and died. That is why I want to stick up for myself and then everything is all right.

I: He just stood there and let them stab him.

T: Amjad was walking down the street and this White, about 16 years old, just started to hit him and punch him and he had all these scabs and cuts all over him. When he came to school nobody believed him. All the white people didn't believe him.

THE RESPONSES OF TEACHERS

In all three schools the headteachers were known by the children to deal firmly with racist incidents. The policy was publicised mainly in the form of responses to specific incidents, often referred to in assembly. This policy was strongly supported by the black children. In general they felt that it had an effect. Bindi thought that as a result of the policy at Woodshire school racist name-calling was decreasing.

> B: I think . . . like in this school they've stopped it because if they keep saying it they can tell the teachers, but the teachers just say 'Don't say it again' and that is probably why they are cutting it down. But if they keep saying then they tell Mr W. Then it will get smaller and smaller . . . When they get to Mrs A's class if you call someone a name she will sort them out. She tells people off. She don't like telling them 'Don't say it again' but she really shouts and she scares you a bit . . . . It will probably get smaller and smaller and then will stop completely.

At Hillside school Rafaqat told us how a boy had been sent to the head for calling him racist names.

> Mr H told him off and Mr H said 'If you do it again you're going to get suspended' and he never did it again.

Greenshire school had the strongest policy in terms both of action taken and of presentation to the pupils. We were talking to a black boy, Johan, and a white friend, Sally.

> Int: This school seems to have an important rule about calling racist names. Does everybody know about it?

> J: Yes, everybody.

> Int: How does everybody know?

> J: They tell them in assembly. Like Fridays all the people come into the hall and Mrs G tells us then like 'I don't want anybody calling anybody racist names' or 'We've got a new rule in the school – no racist names'.

> S: And when somebody calls a person a racist name she says it again in assembly. 'I've told you once. I won't tell you twice.'

The black children all thought that the head took effective action. Bhupinder gave us an example.

> B: Some people get into big serious trouble for calling racist names.

> Int: In this school?

B: Yes, very big trouble. This boy called Colin and Dian she's black and she wanted the rubber and he goes 'I don't let black people borrow, I only let white' and she started crying and Mrs G heard. She said 'If you say that again you're out this school'. She won't put up with it. Mrs G don't put up with sexism as well. She hates it.

Int: Do you think all the children here in our class understand that?

B: Yes.

Raj and Jagdeep told us of another incident. We had asked if there was much racist name-calling.

R: Not much.

J: Because Mrs G, we tell Mrs G and she gets them told off and she writes a letter sometimes. Sometimes in dinner time they get a red card.

R: You know Martin, he's been annoying us the most, he used to call racist names the most and now he's had a warning by Mrs G and if he calls out names again to us he will be expelled.

Sundeep and Akwinder explained the effect of the threat.

Int: Did that stop him?

S: Yes, it stopped him.

A: He's still naughty though.

S: But he ain't racist any more to me.

White children in general in all three schools also regarded the policy as effective. They were particularly clear about it at Greenshire school. This is Leanne and Chris.

L: It used to happen, but now everybody has stopped calling.

C: It's because Miss G had a word with us when somebody called Jagdeep 'Bobble 07' and Jagdeep went to tell to Miss G and she had a word with the class to stop calling people names.

C: She said she would bring your parents in and if you kept on doing it after that she would probably tell you to move to a different school.

Some of the white children described how the policy had affected their behaviour. This is Samantha, who was telling us that sometimes she got mad with Asian children.

Int: And then you say racist things, or you think racist things?

S: I think racist, I don't say them.

Int: So what sort of things do you think?

S: I don't know really. Feel like saying 'You don't own this country'. Things like that.

Int: Do you mean that people like that don't really belong in this country or what?

S: No not that, it's just that they get you mad. They get you too mad sometimes and you feel like saying something to them.

Int: What, something that would hurt them?

S: Yes, but you daren't.

Int: Why don't you?

S: I'd get told off.

In all three schools the promulgation and the implementation of the policy was heavily reliant on the head. Many black children were critical of the failure of class teachers to take effective action. They were also critical of lunchtime supervisors for not responding to racist behaviour. Their role was often even more crucial than that of teachers, because racist incidents often tended to occur during the midday break. The failure of staff to act effectively undermined the validity of the case put by the school, against the position of many parents, that children shouldn't respond to racist name-calling by hitting back but instead should tell a teacher.

Kevin at Hillside school told us about a boy who called him racist names.

He's about the toughest so we can't try to beat him in, so you just have to leave it at that or tell the teacher. But most of the teachers don't do nothing about it.

He gave an example (with Steven, a white friend) of a boy who often called him names like 'nigger'.

Int: What can you do about it?

K: Well sometimes I fight him off, sometimes I tell the teacher.

Int: What does the teacher do?

S: She just keeps telling him to go to different places. Telling Kevin to stay away from him.

How did children, black and white, interpret the failure of teachers and playground supervisors to deal with racism? One explanation was that they didn't have sufficient authority over children to stop their racist behaviour, Kevin explained to us that children would only take notice of the head.

K: He's more tougher on them, so they would listen. It stops for a bit and then starts again. But with the ordinary teachers, talk to them, it starts straight after.

Some children thought that staff's lack of action showed that they were biased against black children. Not only did they not deal with racist incidents, they tended to blame black children more than white children. This view was held by a number of the white children we spoke to as well as some of the black children. In a discussion at Woodshire school with Imran and Amjad and two white girls, Tina and Gemma, the two boys were talking about instances where they felt the teacher had discriminated against them. The two White girls provide a commentary which places those instances in the general context of racist discrimination in society. (Tina confuses a country she visited with a programme she saw.)

I: If there is a black and white person fighting I know that the black person gets told off.

Int: Is that so, why is that?

T: Once Imran was pretend fighting and Miss came up to him and Miss told him off and he had to stand outside . . .

G: I watched a programme and it had these white people got on a bus and this black person wanted to get on the bus and the bus driver shouted 'No you can't get on the bus, all the white people have to go on' and they pushed him out of his own country.

Int: Really, why did that happen?

T: It happened in a country where I went, I think it was Spain. A black driver and white people on a bus and they were standing in a queue and all the white people got on and then this black lady came along with this black man and the driver says 'No sorry this bus is only for white people'. They had to catch another one.

Int: Really.

G: I know, it's America and there was a new law made that all the white people are entitled to the bus but if there are some white people waiting by the bus and there are some black people and they wanted to get on they wouldn't let them get on the bus, they had to walk.

A: There was this boy, Karl, I was fighting and he never got done for that, sent to Mr W and everything.

Int: Really, was it your fault?

A: No. We were playing football and I accidentally kicked him in his leg and he started punching and I got him down and he started crying and Miss came and took me in.

Int: Amjad is saying that white teachers might stick up for white children more than black children.

G: Yes, because sometimes they think that black people cause more trouble than white people.

What was interpreted by some children as racist bias against black children was seen by other children as part of a more general tendency of teachers and supervisors not to deal effectively with any incidents of conflict behaviour, as this extract from a discussion with Kevin and a white friend, Steven, illustrates.

K: When I go and tell Mrs P she just says 'Just go away please' and it's sort of like favouritism to the white people. Sort of like that.

Int: Do you think that she tells you to go away but if you were white she wouldn't?

K: I feel like that, but . . .

Int: Do you think that might be true what Kevin says that Mrs P shows favouritism?

S: No, because I get told to go away for being a pain.

Many children expressed the same view, Sarah, a white girl at Hillside school, began by describing an incident of boys calling Ghazala, a black girl in the class, racist names.

S: They'll call her names. She won't take it too hard at first but then they'll start getting really nasty about it and she'll just go and start crying and go off, and she'll grass on them.

Int: To the teacher?

S: Yes. And then they'll get done. Like the teacher will say 'Oh stop telling tales' because they don't really understand.

Int: How do you mean, 'they don't really understand'?

S: Say they've been picking on you and you go up and tell them, they'll say 'Oh stop telling tales' and they won't believe you and they won't do nothing about it, so when you go and play what you're doing they'll come again and they'll start picking on you. So you go to tell the teacher and they say 'Oh stop it will you'. They tell us to stop it and you haven't even done nothing, but it's not very often that you go grassing to the teacher any more.

Int: Why not?

S: Because it's not worth it.

Int: Do you think the teachers don't understand that you do get upset about it, or do you think they think that you should just sort it out among yourselves even if you do get upset?

S: They think we should sort it out among ourselves.

Int: Do you think that sometimes it would be better if the teachers did stop it happening.

S: Yes, because there wouldn't be half as many children crying and getting upset.

Some children, like Sarah, had concluded from their experience that it was a waste of time telling teachers about anything. As Leanne at Greenshire school said: 'I don't tell teachers because I've been learnt since infants at my old school every time you try and tell the teacher they say "Stop telling tales".'

Many children told us that the most important thing that teachers could do, and the precondition for effective action, was to listen to children who felt that they were being unfairly treated, whether on racist or other grounds. We asked Kevin what he would like teachers to do to stop racist name-calling.

K: Well I would like them to pay more attention and try to stop all the bullying in school and all the name-calling.

Int: How could they do that then? What is the best thing they could do to stop that?

K: Listen. Don't know any more.

Int: What do you think should happen to people that do call racist names?

K: Sent to Mr H.

Int: And what do you think he should do?

K: Well just tell them off and if they do it again suspend them. But if it's not all that bad, just tell them off.

Children who had broken school rules, including that against racist name-calling, also appreciated teachers who listened to them. The effectiveness of the head of Greenshire school was not due only to a well-known firm policy and punitive measures. She was also very skilful at knowing how to deal with particular children. Sometimes she shouted at them, but often she talked to them and listened to them, as Katy, a white girl who had used racist name-calling, describes.

Int: You were saying that teachers don't listen, but you also said that except Miss G . . .

K: She listens. If I did something wrong, if someone shouted at me and was really nasty I think I would be too worried about them shouting at me, I wouldn't be really be learning the lesson, but if someone sits down and talks to you and talks it out I really listen. Once I got sent down to Miss G and she talked with me because we had a fight me and Jagdeep and I told the truth. We both told the truth, he told Miss G what he said and I told her what I said, because I never tell lies because I know I've tried it. When I told a lie it got worst and worst. I told Miss G because if you tell the truth you get in less trouble and so I told the truth and I told her I was sorry with Jagdeep and we said sorry to each other. She talked, and if you did tell lies she would shout but I always tell the truth now.

Int: So what happened between you and Jagdeep?

K: Well we were doing Book Club and I said 'Can you all get out please because we're going to start' and he goes 'Shut up Fatty, Big Gob' so people call him 'Bobble 07' because you know he's got a bobble on his head, so I didn't know what to say and I got upset about it. So I didn't know what I was saying and then I just said it out and he told Miss G, and she told me off but very, very calmly and she's dead nice. She doesn't shout but if you don't tell the truth and tell lies she might get a bit angry, but if you tell the truth she will talk to you. I don't like teachers that shout because I'm too worried about them shouting.

IS THE POLICY FAIR?

The white children generally agreed with the school having a policy against racist name-calling, but their views differed about the justification for treating it more severely than other forms of name-calling. The greatest dissatisfaction was voiced at Greenshire school, the school which laid the greatest emphasis on its policy on racist name-calling in comparison both with the other schools and with other forms of name-calling. Gillian thought it was right because racist names caused more hurt than other names.

Int: Is that how it is at this school? That that is something that the school is very strict about?

G: Yes, very, very strict. With Miss G, if you just said 'Paki' or something like that you'd get into bad trouble.

Int: What if you said another name that wasn't a racist name, would you still get in the same trouble?

G: What, like 'Dickhead' or something like that?

Int: You wouldn't get in the same . . .?

G: No.

Int: Why do you think you would get into such a lot more trouble for saying a name about somebody's colour or something than to say another sort of name?

G: I don't know really, it's just horrible, like if I call someone 'Dickhead' it doesn't really hurt them, but if I call someone a 'black bastard', something like that, it would hurt them.

Int: So you think it is right that the school should be so strict about that?

G: Yes.

But some children, like Martin, who had been in trouble for racist name-calling, didn't understand why the head was so much more strict about racist names. He was talking about what would happen if a boy used a non-racist name.

M: He wouldn't get told off then. No, because half of the school call names like 'Big Mouth' and 'Pig' and 'Cow' and all that stuff. She knows why because that is they're picking on them, which they always call 'Pig' and 'Cow'.

Int: So why does Miss G get very annoyed if you say something like 'Chocolate' or a name about people's colour, but doesn't get annoyed if you say 'Pig' or 'Big Mouth' or something like that?

M: I don't know.

Because they didn't see a reason for the singling out of racist name-calling, many of the white children didn't think it was fair. Their objection was not to racist name-calling being strictly punished, but to other, non-racist, name-calling not being. They saw the policy as in contradiction to the principle of equality. Some white children saw this as unfair because they were themselves the victims of name-calling which upset them just as much as black children were by racist name-calling. A case in point was Michelle, who was persecuted more than any other child in the two top classes at Greenshire school – sometimes by black children.

Int: Why do you think Miss G was so annoyed at people calling racist names? Was she more annoyed at that than other names that people call?

M: She was. They've got rights haven't they in this country as well. She's always saying things about racist name-calling but she really has a go at them. I don't know why.

Int: I wonder why?

M: I don't know why.

Int: Do you think that calling people names about their colour is worse than calling them other names or not worse? Like calling you things to do with fleas?

M: I don't know because Miss G seems to think so. Miss G says it's worse, she never says why.

Int: Do you think that somebody who calls a name like 'Paki' or 'Chocolate', those sorts of names, that they should get into more trouble than somebody who calls you things about 'fleas'?

M: I don't know really, I think it should be the same, because I mean they should have equal rights. If they get called things, and we get called things by them, not just 'white ice-cream', they call me 'Fleas' and stuff. Rajvinder he calls me 'Fleas'. Because I used to call him a racist name and I got battered by Miss G, and then he just calls me 'Fleas' and Miss G don't do anything about it, but she really told me off for calling him a racist name. I think Miss G thinks it is a lot more worse than just 'Fleas' and stuff.

Int: But you don't?

M: No.

Int: Do you have any idea why Miss G does?

M: I don't know. I mean everyone keeps picking on them and saying things but she never says why she is so mad about it.

The apparent unfairness of the policy to some children arose most acutely over instances of black children calling white children racist names. We asked Katherine what would happen in such a case.

K: Let's say like if Miss G found out that the black people had been saying 'white ice-cream', I don't think that she would say anything, but if we called someone 'Paki' or 'Bobble 07' – because everyone used to called Jagdeep that. [Miss G] stopped everyone from saying that because he got upset for that, because he had to do it for his religion, I don't know. If anyone says that, what you said, I don't think that it would be as bad as people calling 'Paki'. I don't know why. I can't really explain because if they say it to us, I don't think it will make any difference because it's just a name that is. If say I called Mandeep a 'Paki' and she called me a 'white ice-cream', I think the teacher would go on about me calling her a 'Paki' rather than her calling me a 'white ice-cream'.

Int: But supposing you were just as upset as she was, would that make any difference?

K: I think that they would still go – well they would calm the white person down.

Int: Do you think that is fair?

K: Yes, because it wouldn't be fair if they told the white person off for calling them 'Paki'. It wouldn't be fair it they told the black person off for calling 'white ice-cream'. I think they should tell both off.

Int: But in this school, if a white person called a black person a name would you get into more trouble?

K: Yes I think you would.

Int: Is that fair do you think?

K: No, because I think that you should both be treated the same way. Because some people treat white people better than black people, and some people treat black people better than white people.

Scott saw the policy as a denial of the equal rights of white British people.

Int: Why do you think the school is very strict on white people calling racist names, but not the other way round? Why do you think it is like that?

S: Because if say somebody called an Indian in this school, they would tell their dad and they would get onto the council and call this school sexist probably. It's not fair.

Int: Do you think there shouldn't be a rule about calling names and it's all right to call people names about their colour, or what?

S: It isn't right to call people names about their colour.

Int: Why not?

S: Well it's like saying something about your religion. It's their future, they're used to it. Not fair is it?

Int: So what's wrong with having a strict rule about that then?

S: Well we've got a culture as well. Say if we call their culture we get told off, but if they insult ours they don't.

Scott suggested that some teachers and other staff were actually biased against white children.

The trouble is with some of the teachers and some of the dinner ladies and most of the teachers, say if we called somebody coloured a name but if somebody coloured called us a name they don't get told off. They believe them, so we get into trouble for lying even though we are telling the truth.

'RACE IN THE CURRICULUM

At the three schools, most of the children said they had done little or no work in lessons on issues of 'race'. The general view among black and white children was that it would be a good idea. This was Bindi's view at Woodshire school.

Int: Do you think that there are lots of things to do with black people that white children here ought to know about?

B: Yes, about how we used to live and all that. Like we have history here of England, but there is no other history, it's all about English, all the white people and I think they should have history – there should be an Indian man who can talk English who knows quite a lot about all this stuff and can teach you about all of this in one of the classes. I don't really know who could do that.

Int: Is that your idea or have you got an older brother or sister or something who said . . .?

B: No it's just my idea, I just thought it up now.

Int: Do you think that it would have to be an Indian person to teach about those things or could a white person do it?

B: If an English person knew, they could probably teach them.

Int: Why do you think teaching those things would be a good idea?

B: To know how the Indian – because some people think that Indian people are bad people, but if they knew how they used to live they would probably change their minds and stop calling us all these things.

Jane, a white girl in the same class, thought that there should be lessons explicitly about immigration and racism, and this would reduce racist name-calling in the class.

J: Well we've had religion, but not about racism, and about why people come here.

Int: Do you think it would be a good idea to have lessons about these things or not?

J: Yes, because some people don't really know what they are saying so we should really find out why these people come over and then they will know and they won't call people 'Blackies' and things and they will realise that they can come

over just like we go over there, so why should we be racist to
them because they're not to us.

Charlotte at Hillside school thought there should be lessons in which
black children were able to explain how racist name-calling made
them feel.

If they knew how Asian children and Jamaican children felt, if an
Asian child and a Jamaican child were allowed to stand up and tell
them how they felt, how people call them names like 'Blackie' and
things like that, I think they would stop it.

At Greenshire school the children said they had done nothing on
'race' in the classroom, though they did tell us about doing work on
personal relationships: on conflict and on sexism. They had, however,
had assemblies about racism in children's relationships.

Raising issues of 'race' in the curriculum could, however, create
problems for black children, as some of them pointed out to us.
Kevin, an Afro-Caribbean boy at Hillside school, told us how when
his teacher referred to Africa during a lesson there was a moment of
embarrassment for him, though he felt that it was worth it in order
to challenge white prejudice.

K: When Mrs L wrote 'Africa' on the board and I think she said
      something about the black man, everybody turned round and
      looked at me. I didn't look at them though. I just put my face
      down.

Int: Did you? Did that embarrass you?

K: Yes.

Int: Do you think that you would rather she didn't mention things
      like that because then it wouldn't embarrass you?

K: Yes and no, because I want people to stop thinking that this
      is white people's land and I want them to stop thinking 'my
      land is white'. I've forgotten the 'no'.

Int: The 'no' I suppose is for also you don't like the embarrass-
      ment. So how would you weigh up the two of them, would
      you say 'Well I would rather, even if it embarrassed me
      sometimes, I would still rather the teacher did it because it
      is important they learn about it'?

K: Yes.

Chapter 9

The four girls

Up to now we have looked at a number of aspects of the racialisation of children's cultures, drawing on extracts from discussions from a large number of children across the three schools. One important indication of the significance of the issues we have identified is that they have arisen in the experiences of numbers of children and in all three schools. However, we do not want to lose sight of the fact that these issues are represented in specific combinations in the life-worlds of each child, in their relationships, their social identities, their interaction repertoires, and their worldviews. To separate out the various elements that make these up is necessary in order to analyse and understand them, but it is also important to see how they come together for the individual child.

For that reason we want to end our empirical exploration by devoting this chapter to the lives of four girls, Yvette, Natasha, Hayley and Rebecca. These four formed a a group of best friends in Woodshire school. Yvette was Afro-Caribbean, Natasha's parents were Afro-Caribbean and white, Hayley and Rebecca were white. We have chosen these four because their lives embodied many of the themes that we have identified, often very graphically, and because they were particularly articulate in discussing them with us. For those reasons we spent more time in discussion with them than with any other children. 'Race' was a significant factor in their relationships, both those within the group and those with other children outside it, in numerous ways. It was a dimension of their relationships with other children, with teachers, with their parents, with older brothers and sisters, and with other adults. In the following section we want to try and describe the complex web of social relationships that made up their social world, and in particular the racialised aspects of it that they talked about.

Why were they friends? We asked this when we first talked to Hayley and Rebecca.

H: We know a lot about each other. We can understand each other, like Rebecca's dad and mum have split up and my dad has split and Yvette's mum split up, so we can understand each other.

Int: Do you talk to each other about those things?

H: Yes. . . . We trust each other. . . . It's understanding. You can understand their way and they can understand the way you feel.

We asked if there was any other reason.

R: We just mess about.

Int: What does messing about mean?

H: Have a laugh.

R: Because Yvette and Natasha are dead funny and really make you laugh.

H: They like act things and you're stood there laughing your socks off.

Their answer summed up two key elements in their relationship: the enjoyment of just being together, messing around, having a laugh, and the psychological intimacy that they shared. We should add that Natasha shares their common experiences of family background: her father died quite recently. Nearly a year after we first met them, when we knew them quite well, we asked them this.

Int: You have lots of arguments but you're still friends. Do you think it is more difficult for you four to be friends because two of you are black and two of you are white?

All: No.

Int: Or do you think that if you were four black girls or four white girls it would be just the same?

R: I'd say if we were all black girls or all white girls we'd argue more.

Y: We like each other because we talk to each other and you can tell that these two aren't racist and we're not prejudiced because we're half-caste and black.

H: It's better for us because like Yvette is black and Natasha is half-caste and us two are white and so you don't go criticising the black people because you know you'll be talking about one of your best friends.

They saw the mixed nature of their group as a positive feature, which had engendered a shared anti-racism and trust between the black girls and the white girls. Perhaps the feeling of how meaningful they felt the achievement of a multi-racial close friendship group was, in a world that they all saw as full of racism, is brought out in this extract.

N: When I used to go in this pub with my mum and there used to be loads of white people and then it was just me, just the coloured person, I feel like different. I had to go where my mum works yesterday and I was surrounded by white people because my mum is sitting next to me and all these people were staring at me and I didn't know where to look and people kept on going like that at me. I just felt different.

Int: Does that surprise you Rebecca?

R: No, I can understand it but I don't think the colour really matters. We're all the same underneath but people just get carried away sometimes. I mean people think that all the black people have all the Rottweilers and start all the fights. Like the police think it is the black people, not the white people.

N: When you go in the pub those big guys who think they're ace, and you walk in a pub and you're really looking scared, they look at you really horrible, like mean and going to beat you up and that, and when you suddenly start to walk out the door they sort of like walk up to you and say 'Where do you think you're going' and if you watched one of those films where white people and black coloured people are fighting, like *Police Academy*. If you watch the film it was where this one black coloured man was in the army and people wouldn't let him go in the shower, all the men were in the shower, he had to wait last. And then when he went in the shower the white people started cutting him in the back with a knife and this white person started sticking up for him, his best

friend. This white person tried to push them off the top of
the house and he never fell because his best friend was there
and then when everyone was asleep everyone came in his
bedroom while other people were asleep and they took him
to this place where they call him horrible names like 'You're
not the same as us white people'. I was going to have tears
down my eyes because of what they were saying to him. I
was thinking how tight it was to pick on coloured people
and coloured people pick on white people, because I used
to say to Yvette 'We're all the same, we've got a heart, we've
got a brain, we've eyes, we've got ears. It's just that we are
different colours' and me and Yvette, the white people just
used to call us horrible names and that.

CONFLICTS WITH OTHER CHILDREN

The most striking feature of the accounts that the four girls gave us
of what happened in their daily lives was the centrality of conflict.
Their stories almost always revolved around arguments with other
children, sometimes ebullient exchanges and escapades, sometimes
involving heated tempers, name-calling and fighting. In school, most
of this took place within the large network of girls from the two
sixth year classes who played together. It was during these heated
arguments that racist name-calling mostly took place, as Natasha
describes.

N: Lisa was crying one day. There was me, Yvette and Becky
[Rebecca]. We had an argument and because we had a
row with Julie as well. Julie kept on calling me and Yvette
'Niggers' and everything and I just felt like calling her a name
back. When she started calling us a name again we just said
'Milky Bar' or something and when Lisa Wild started crying
she got more people started crowding round her because she
was crying.

[. . .]

N: When she started crying she had loads of attention and then
she told Mr N and then all four of them what were standing
up behind the seat, then more people crammed round us to
get more people on her side and we got more people on our
side. They just started telling a pack of lies because she says

that I thumped her in the stomach, Yvette pulled her hair, Hayley kicked her in the shin and Becky started mouthing off and everything. And Gurjit started crying because they was all talking about dads and everyone . . .

Y: No, Lisa called Gurjit a 'Paki'. Gurjit was crying, and when I went up and said 'Look what you've done to her.'

(Natasha says that Gurjit was upset by remarks about her father because he had been sent to prison for drunken driving.)

Among the most frequent sources of conflict situations were the relay races that the girls, together with some of the boys, organised every break-time in the playground. Girls might be accused of being big-headed and showing off if they won, or being mardy if they lost. Just as the races themselves were competitive arenas for displaying physical qualities, so the accompanying disputes were social arenas for displaying skill in conflictual social interaction. As Yvette put it, other girls 'start being mouthy and think they're hard'. It is important to recognise how strongly affected the girls were by these disputes. In talking about them, words like 'explode' and 'burst out' often occurred. This is Rebecca.

I get really wound up over races when another team has cheated and they call you all names and they come up to you and push you, and you push them all back and there is a great explosion between them. I get really wound up when I've done races. I'm in a mood all day because I just can't stand it like.

The principal social function of these disputes was to renegotiate the relationships among the group of girls by allowing them to reveal their real feelings and attitudes to each other in an atmosphere of heightened emotions. On one occasion, after the four girls had been telling me stories of arguments they had been involved in, we asked them if they enjoyed them. Yvette said 'Yes, I love them. It's natural to have arguments because if you didn't have arguments then it would just be a boring life'. She continued: 'It's always your friends right and they are getting on your nerves and you want to say something you can't so when you break friends with them you can tell everything you just let it out "I hate you". I really like arguments that's why. And if you want to cry you just go in the loos'.

These arguments sometimes led to racist name-calling. According to Yvette. 'Most of the time it happens at playtime, like when we play games like relays and they say "No you never won, Blackies" or something like that.'

One incident of racist name-calling over who won occurred in the toilets after a rounders game. According to Natasha, 'We all got in a row and Sharon and Tina were calling us "Niggers" and "Blackies"'. Tina and Yvette agreed to talk to us together about this incident. Yvette said:

Y: We were good friends before but it's very difficult now.

Int: How did you feel when she said that?

Y: Sad. Angry.

Int: Tell me about both of those, why were you angry and why were you sad?

Y: I was sad because she called me a name about my colour and I was angry because I didn't think she would say anything like that before. She hasn't said anything like that to me before.

Tina explained that she thought saying 'nigger' was the same as saying 'silly cow' to a white girl. Yvette disagreed. She said that she didn't take non-racist names as seriously as racist names because 'if she says something about me it's like they are offending my family as well'. Tina said she was surprised that racist names were particularly upsetting to Yvette. 'I was surprised because sometimes she is a tough girl and she seems to take it.'

How can we explain this incident? Hayley and Rebecca put it like this.

H: I don't think she meant to say it, it's just people get worked up and they just want to say something. Like because people call you names you have to say something back because you can't just stand there and let people call you names but I don't think Tina meant it because Tina and Yvette used to be very good best friends.

R: It's just like you have to let everything out like sometimes you feel like getting dead hot and you have to let everything out when you go outside and you just feel like saying something that will hurt. You just get all these feelings out and explode if somebody says something nasty to you.

In another discussion with Yvette and Natasha they talked about Tina and others making racist remarks such as 'go back to your own country' and we asked them how they thought they meant it.

N: They just want to hurt us.

Y: To get at us.

Racist name-calling was a tactic to achieve interactional dominance in the immediate situation, but its social power within children's interaction derived, as they recognised, from its trading on racialised power relations in the wider society.

Int: Why do you think children do call you racist names sometimes, why do they do it?

Y: My mum always tells me that they're jealous.

N: Those who do it though they make the best of it because there's more people white than black in England so they can call you whatever they like.

Underlying the incident between Tina and Yvette were two social processes involving dominance. One was competition between the children over who won the rounders game. But intertwined with that, according to Tina, was competition over friendship relations between her, Yvette and Natasha. In the subsequent discussion with Yvette and Tina, Tina said that she wouldn't call Yvette racist names again but that she might to other children if they had an argument. We asked Yvette how she felt about that, and she said that it would matter to her because a racist remark affected all black people (as she said in another context, 'when you insult another black person that means you are insulting me as well'). Tina then said 'That's why I called Yvette a nigger instead of Natasha, because I wanted to hurt Natasha instead of Yvette'. She explained that she hadn't said this to Natasha directly because she knew that Natasha would tell the teacher, whereas Yvette wouldn't, but she knew that Natasha would be offended by her calling racist names to Yvette. Yvette confirmed that 'she was as offended as me'. Tina went on to explain how Natasha was jealous of her friendship with Yvette. We don't know to what extent Tina was trying, in giving an account after the event in a discussion with Yvette, to avoid blame. Yvette seemed to find her explanation acceptable, and acknowledged that Natasha was jealous and did try to 'stir it up a bit'. Without going any deeper into the detail of the incident, it is clear that it took place in two contexts of competition and dominance. One was the situation of competition over the result of the game. The other was competition over best-friend relationships among Tina, Yvette and Natasha.

The racialisation of interaction in school needs to be seen as part of wider histories of relationships in the local community. Yvette lived only a few doors away from Tina. When we returned to their school and talked to Yvette some six months after the previous incident, she told us of another incident with Tina that had happened in the meantime.

Y: Her little sister – she's been teaching her little sister to swear, right, and she called me a 'Black B', right.

Int: Who did?

Y: Tina's little sister, she's only 6 years old, right. Tina's been teaching her all the swear words, so she come to me calling me racist names and all that lot and she kicked me about ten times. I goes 'Emma don't kick me again because I'll kick you back because you're getting on my nerves', so she kicked me, I kicked her back, I got done.

R: You can't just let a little girl come up to you and kick you and everything and you're just expected to stand there. Just because she's little. It would be all right if it was someone say your age because you could hit them back as hard, but when a little girl comes up to you, if you hit them back – I mean you get angry, yes, and if you hit them back you get done. But I mean you've got to hit them back or something.

Yvette told us that Tina had complained to her mother, who had told Yvette off, and to her class teacher, who had told Tina 'Your sister is a little stirrer as well, isn't she?'

We have seen how Yvette and Natasha reacted strongly to racist name-calling. As Rebecca put it, 'Yvette just gets really wound up if any one calls her names . . . She gets totally wound up and she'll have a go at them. She'll hit them'. Hayley added 'When she's in a mood then I would stay out of her way'. The sub-culture of the two black girls contained a number of features which addressed problems such as racist name-calling. Perhaps the most important was the value they gave to 'sticking up for yourself'. This entailed the ability to 'take it' or to 'handle it'; in other words to be able to cope with verbal or physical aggression from other children, Yvette remembered that 'I used to cry all the time but I don't any more. Since fourth year, everyone was picking on me, I started sticking up for myself'. The need to 'be tough' was illustrated rather graphically by an incident involving Natasha and her older brother, Yvette began the story.

> Tina was really scared because she thought Natasha would hit her and beat her up and Tina goes 'Yes I want a fight', so we went to this kind of square thing and they were having a fight. Tina was pulling Natasha's hair. Natasha nearly started crying and then Natasha got up, Tina was getting beat up and she had all scars on her legs and everything and she had a big bump. . . . Tina hit her and then her brother came over and he goes 'You lost you divvy' and kicked her.

Natasha explained.

> N: When I was having a fight with Tina my brother was there and then when I got up my brother kicked me in the stomach and then he made me cry and I was crying in the night.
>
> Int: Why did he do that?
>
> N: Because he saw I lost the fight.

The opposite of 'being tough' was children who acted tough but in situations of conflict cried in order to get other children on their side, or to gain the sympathy of teachers, Yvette told us about an argument they had with a white girl, Lisa.

> She just cried to get her own way. She cries to get attention, and everyone is going on her side except us because we're like the tough ones. We know what she's like.

There was a strong sense of solidarity between Yvette and Natasha.

> N: Well we just stick up for ourselves sometimes, and when Yvette starts crying I'm always going up to the person and saying 'Leave her alone'.
>
> Y: If they hit Natasha you can't help but hit them back. I've got to. Imran, he kicked Natasha and he made a bruise, so I went back to him the next day and kicked him on the shin.

Their reputation for being tough deterred some children from calling them racist names, but led them into competitive situations with others where racist name-calling occurred.

Y: Well some of our friends won't call us names because they know that we'll start getting at them harder and everything, but not-friends start being mouthy and think they're hard, they think they can beat us at races like Carla and Emma.

Their toughness had come from the experience of being harassed by white children when they were younger. Their experience in the infant school had shown them the value of mutual support among black children. As Natasha said, 'because we were all tough, all the black ones, it never troubled us'. They said that they missed the lack of a supporting network of black children at their present school. Yvette said that she thought things would be better at the secondary school. Natasha agreed.

N: Yes, because if anyone hits me or Yvette there is my brother and my cousin to stick up for us and if Anita [Yvette's older cousin] is still there she'll stick up for me and Yvette as well.

Y: She's left school. You feel safe when someone is our friend, older than us, you feel safe then.

HAYLEY AND REBECCA

We want to turn now to the two white girls in the group. We will begin by looking at their general views about racism. In several conversations they talked about how they understood racism. The following extracts come from discussions with just the two of them.

Int: Some people say that 'there are too many black people in this country' and that 'they should go back' and that sort of thing. What do you think of that?

R: I think people shouldn't say that. I think the other coloured person should just be able to do what they like in this country the same as anybody else because they are only a different colour. Like a coloured boy and a white boy are just the same and a coloured girl and a white girl are just the same, so I think people who say that shouldn't say it because if they want to come into this country they're welcome in this

country, but some people don't welcome them with open
arms.

H: Yes, people are prejudiced. They think that black people
should be in black countries but if you think about it white
people go to other places, like Spain. We took over Australia
so it's just the same, but they live here, they want to stay here
so it's up to them really.

And again:

Int: Do you think that black and white people are treated the
same in this country?

H: No.

R: No.

Int: What's the difference?

H: White people are more popular in this country and black
people tend to be the ones who have Rottweiler dogs and
all things like that, and the police tend to think that it is the
black people in this country that are the cause for all the
trouble, because if you looked at a white man and then a
black man you'd think the black man was a trouble-maker,
but it isn't really. The white people are more trouble-makers
than the black.

R: Because the black look more like big and they look more
stronger than the white men because they've got a better
build, and I think it's because black people came to this
country and the Whites started it off and I think the people
ever since think that they invaded our country, but really we
invaded them first.

Int: How do you mean?

R: Like they all came over here but really they came over here
because we went over there first. We went to Pakistan and
things like that first, so they came over here, and ever since
people have held it against them. It was their fault that they
come over here but really it's our fault.

We wanted to find out how they came to think like this.

Int: How do you know these things? Did you have lessons about it here?

R: No, my mum and my dad. Because my real dad used to tell me things but then my mum told me loads of things and then my step-dad knows quite a few things and he tells me, and I just remember them.

Int: And are these things that they talk to you about?

H: It's things that you find out when you're walking down the street, like you can walk in the town and there's a black man walking and there's a white man calling a black man 'Paki', so that's one reason that you learn about it, and just by thinking about it you know really why the black people think that the white people shouldn't call them names because the white people are like stingy to the black people but the black people don't mind at all. They think that white men are just like the black men, they're all together in a group, but the white people think well it's a fight against them, it's a white team and a black team, and they think there should be a fight over it.

R: And you learn these things like if you are walking down a road with your mum, like going to a paper shop or something like that, and there's a group of black people there and you goes 'Why are there black people?' and you just bring up the subject and then she will tell you. You say 'Why are there loads of black people?' and she says 'Well I don't really know how it all started, but I know we invaded their country and they came back and some stayed over there. Then the black people came over to our country and ever since we've just like been black and white'.

They had some interesting things to say about racism in everyday interaction. Here they demonstrate their understanding of teenage peer culture and group pressures, and changes over time. The extract begins with them talking about black people.

R: I feel sorry for them because my sister was saying things about them and my mum goes to her 'Well they're just the same people inside, it doesn't matter what they are on the outside' and I goes 'Yes mum I agree with you about that', because older sisters, about 19, tend to say things like that don't they?

H: 'Those Blackies' or 'I'm fed up with them Pakis'.

R: My sister says that. Like 'Half-caste' like Imran and Amjad, like my sister says 'I'm fed up with them Pakis'.

Int: How old are your sisters?

H: 12.

R: 19.

Int: Are you saying that older people are more likely to say those things?

R: Yes, like when they get to age about 25 then they realise.

H: It's round about the teenager age when they tend to say it more. I know the children say it, they say it quite a lot, but the older people say it more, I don't know why, but if you are walking in the town and there is a coloured person and there's boys like aged 14 and 15 walk past and call them 'Pakis'.

R: It's when they are about 13. When they get to about 24 they stop saying it. My mum used to say it when she was a teenager but then she realised that we are all the same underneath.

Int: Did she? How do you know?

R: Because she told me. I was in the third year or fourth year and I called Imran a Paki, and I went home and told my mum and she said 'You shouldn't call them that because I was a teenager and I called them that, but when you're older you realise what you have said and they are all the same underneath'.

Int: So what is it that happens when you are about 12 or 13 that makes you change?

R: They just think it's funny and call them Pakis.

H: When you get older you realise more what you have been saying. Like when somebody has said something to you you realise how much it feels inside and then you realise what other people have to take.

R: Yes, when they've got their mates with them and they think it is funny because they think they are showing off like Amjad does. If you laugh at him when he is being funny he will do it more. Because they think it's funny because they are with loads of mates, the same age group. Like lads, if you've got loads of boys like about 15 all together, one of will find it funny to do that. And even if one of them doesn't find it funny he won't say nothing.

Int: Why not?

R: Because he thinks everyone else thinks it's funny and they'll think it strange if he says it's wrong.

They saw an important gender difference here. At their age, they thought that the girls did more name-calling than the boys, because the boys just played football while the girls had arguments. This was a view shared by many of the children. But in the secondary school, the girls will have grown out of continual arguing ('they won't be bothered with things like that'), but the boys will do much more name-calling, because they won't be playing football all the time and because they haven't got any feelings – in other words their group culture excludes the reciprocity of perspective that leads girls to empathise with the feelings of those hurt by name-calling.

R: We won't have so many arguments, I don't think there'll be so many names as well. But really at 14, around that age, it tends to be where you do start calling names. Mostly boys. I'm not blaming all the boys but it is mostly boys.

Int: Why is that do you think?

R: I don't know.

Int: Why are boys different from girls about that?

R: They're older and they know what they're saying and they don't care.

Int: Why don't girls do it at that age so much?

N: They've got other things to do. With boys they do get bored and want to do something.

Y: Yes, we get tired of it because they've been doing it a lot at this school.

Int: Have boys been doing it a lot at this school?

Y: It's stupid but more than you do girls.

Int: At this school or older?

Y: Older.

R: At this school boys leave you alone and just say it now and then but at this school girls do say it more. But when they're older I think the boys say it much more. Most probably all the boys that are at this school when they're about 14, they'll be saying it then, because they haven't been saying it here a lot and they'll have the time to do it then, but with the girls they have been saying it here and when they're older they're not going to be bothered with things like that.

Int: Do you think that's true?

Y: Yes. Because at the older schools most of them don't play football any more. They're just bored.

And it was these factors that accounted for why boys rather than girls tended to use racist name-calling at secondary school age.

H: I think that is mostly the time when they call people 'Pakis'.

Int: What, because they get. . .?

H: The teenagers, well the people at the High School, if that happened they tend to just slip out with it, but they're not really bothered about feelings, they just say it. They've said it and they think it is over and done with for them. And then left that person with feelings and that person goes and messes about and don't care less about it.

R: Some black people don't like that, it hurts their feelings. Like half-caste and things like that don't like it because we're just the same and they don't really like it. They've got hurt feelings.

ARGUMENTS WITHIN THE GROUP OF FOUR GIRLS

Relationships among the four girls, like those between the four girls and other children, were full of conflict, often good-natured, but often hurtful. Before focusing on ways in which their relationships

became racialised, we want to give a brief illustration of some of
their characteristic interaction, by referring to a discussion we had
with the four of them in which they were talking about conflicts
among themselves. The topic arose because earlier in the day there
had been an argument between Hayley and Natasha over helping
one of us with something in the classroom.

> H: Well I was helping you and Natasha didn't like it because I
> was helping you and she called me 'Brainbox' and I go 'Shut
> up just because I'm brainer than you' and she goes 'I'm better
> at running than you' and I says 'So what', and then she goes
> 'Shut up' and I goes 'No'. Like that, and then we just burst
> out laughing at each other.

The discussion went on to other incidents of competition between the
four.

> Y: Hayley couldn't do a cart-wheel and I did a cart-wheel in front
> of the whole class and Hayley said that I was showing off, and
> I reckon that she was jealous. And I said to Hayley 'We've all
> got talents' but she goes 'Yes, yes, but at least I don't show off
> with them'.

A great deal of their interaction was concerned with negotiating
the relationships between them. The problem was to maintain a
relatively equal balance between the claims of four self-assertive
individuals. In the example above, Yvette's statement that 'we've all
got talents' implies that it is legitimate to display the ones that you've
got. Hayley's counter-charge is that to show-off is to transgress the
equality principle in the interests of dominance.

Did these conflicts become racialised? On one occasion Rebecca
and Hayley told us that they never used racist name-calling against
Yvette and Natasha.

> R: We've had plenty of arguments but I haven't turned round to
> them and called them black.

> H: We've had loads of arguments because I've been here since I
> was four. We've had loads of arguments but not once have I
> turned round and called them a 'Paki' or anything.

In fact this was not true. In heated arguments Hayley did, according
to the other three.

> R: Hayley is another one that does call Yvette a 'Paki' a lot.

Y: Most of the time, yes, when we break friends.

R: Like Hayley gets carried away when she is fighting Yvette, she will call her something about her colour.

N: She says 'Go back to your own country', and I goes 'This is our own country so you know it's not your country', and me and Yvette used to walk away.

In a discussion we had with Hayley she talked about calling Natasha a racist name and how it happened.

Int: You said how sometimes people say those things just because they get angry and they want to say something that will hurt somebody.

H: Well I don't think they want to say it to hurt somebody, I just think it comes out without – they don't know what they've been saying. I think it just comes out, and they don't understand what they are saying.

Int: Does that ever happen to you?

H: Yes, that's happened to me before.

R: I've never called Yvette or Natasha 'Paki'.

H: I did at one time. I was out in the yard and Natasha started to hit me and I just pushed her back and called her 'Paki' because I was really feeling to explode and then I said sorry to her, because I realised what I'd said after.

R: I think I've called somebody. I must have called somebody one but I haven't called Yvette and Natasha. I don't really bother with that.

As Rebecca put it on another occasion, 'the names start coming out, because once you've got them in your mind you can't get rid of them'.

It is in the context of the constant negotiation of relations of equality within the group that we want to look now at the question of the assertion of ethnic identity by Natasha and Yvette. It arose most sharply as a result of some work that their class had been doing on slavery, Rebecca said it began with Yvette.

R: She was saying 'black people are stronger, They've got more power. Black people can fight white people'. And I goes 'No that's wrong' and Yvette started saying 'You used us as slaves and everything' and then I said 'No we never' and she said that we went over there and invaded her country. So anyway after that I said to her 'Why are black people over here then?'

Y: Me and Hayley were writing notes and when I said something she goes 'Yes well I wasn't born then' and then she started swearing to me. I said 'You have to say that because you can't face facts'.

This assertion of black identity has a different meaning for the black and the white children. For Yvette, the point is a statement of positive ethnic identity drawing on black resistance to slavery. For Hayley and Rebecca, it seems that Yvette is blaming them personally for slavery. The historical issue of slavery is being translated from being part of the content of the curriculum to being part of the content of the interpersonal relationships of the children in the class. We can trace the steps in this process. Rebecca explained: 'Yvette goes "We've got the power" and Natasha goes to Mr N: "Mr N, Yvette says she's got the power" '. Yvette wasn't getting on with her work and the teacher said, according to Yvette, 'Get on with your work because you'll lose your power'. The next step was in the continuing debate between Hayley and Yvette, when Hayley called Yvette a slave as a jibe. It seems that this theme was taken up by other children in the playground.

N: One day after that I was in the playground and them was all talking about black people and slaves and everything and then I got a gang of coloured people because Imran kept on saying 'Let's have a war against the white people and the coloured people' and then we was all going around saying 'The Black Power' and then Becky came in and she says . . .

Y: Started it into an argument.

N: And she says 'We never used you as slaves because we weren't born then so I don't know why you're . . .'

Y: Because she couldn't face up to it, she just changed the subject, just like that, because she couldn't face facts.

The exact details of what happened are unclear. This was not the only time that Imran, who enjoyed fighting, had suggested 'Blacks against Whites'. It seems that this project never actually materialised. (The racial character of his plan for a fight between the black children at the school and children at another, largely white, school, was dissipated by the enthusiasm of white children to join in with the black children.) What is significant here is the way in which the assertion of black ethnic identity, because it takes place within the context of children's culture strongly structured by processes of dominance and equality, becomes translated by the white children into the terms of attempted black dominance challenging the fragile equality of their interpersonal relationships.

The incident we have just been looking at raises the question of what 'race' in the curriculum means for children's culture. This was not an isolated instance. In their previous year the class had had a lesson on Martin Luther King. Their teacher had told them how Black people had to stand up on the buses to let white people sit down. Afterwards, in the playground, when Natasha and Yvette were sitting on the bench, some of the white children told them to get up and give up their seats, as a way of asserting dominance within their ongoing competitive peer relations.

Int: Mr S must have done that lesson about Martin Luther King because he wanted white children to understand that it was wrong to treat black people differently, but you're saying it didn't work. The white kids didn't understand it like that?

N: No they didn't take it like that. They took it like they thought they had won, but Mr S meant them to take it like not to treat us that way because we're human beings.

These experiences made Natasha and Yvette unhappy about dealing with issues of 'race' in the curriculum. They thought it would be better not to.

Y: Because it gets on your nerves and the kids just come out and call you names and if you hit them you get into trouble, and it just gets on your nerves. You just feel like hitting them, but if you hit them the teachers don't listen to you anyway.

N: I wouldn't mind really if they talked about the slaves, like the coloured people, and they wouldn't go around spreading things.

They are making an important connection here between the teacher's curriculum role and the teacher's pastoral role. Their implicit criticism is of teachers who deal with issues of 'race' in the curriculum but aren't aware of, or ignore, their consequences within children's relationships. In fact, because the two girls find it difficult to imagine that the teachers may not be aware of something that is so central to their peer relationships, they draw the conclusion that teachers who do deal with issues of 'race' do so because they are racist. Their teacher had just done a topic on Australia which caused them embarrassment because children stared at them and made remarks about Aboriginals. Natasha said that

> When we're doing about Aboriginal people and we tell them that we have been learning about Aboriginals, everybody goes around saying 'Aboriginal' to Yvette.

Natasha compared her teacher unfavourably with the teacher of the parallel class.

> Mr N enjoys doing things like this because Mrs A hadn't done a topic on Aborigines. She's just done a topic on Australia but not on Aborigines because if I was in her class she would know that I would get embarrassed or something like that because people pick on me, and it looks like Mr N enjoys it because he does it all the time.

The reason why their interpretation of the teacher's motives seems so credible to them is because it fits into their more general idea that some teachers, and lunchtime supervisors, were biased against black children. Here they are talking about their class teacher.

N: The only thing that I think is he is a racist is because he always listens to the white people.

Y: Like when this girl she hit me, so I hit her back, right, and she kicked me in the stomach, right, so I went to Mr N and he goes 'You tell me your part first' to the white person, so she told him her part – a pack of lies – and then he goes 'Well it seems that you're the liar then, doesn't it Yvette' and he wouldn't let me say my part. He just goes 'Shut up, shut up, shut up' and he wouldn't let me say my part. And that's what got on my wick.

N: When Mr N lets the white person speak first and lets the coloured person speak last, the white person tells a lot of lies, so Mr N believes it and then we tell the truth about us and he just doesn't believe it. He says 'Well it seems like you're the one who started it and made all this argument happen'.

The four girls give two reasons for being friends: they share common experiences, and they enjoy being together and doing things together – messing around, having a laugh. But there was one area of experience that Hayley and Rebecca could not share in the same way as Yvette and Natasha, and that was the experience of being subject to racism. The everyday social interaction of the four girls with other children, particularly with other girls, was full of conflict, and this was a fertile soil for racist name-calling. The sub-culture of this group of children, with its high level of verbal and physical conflict, generated an ideology of 'toughness', in which 'sticking up for yourself', being able to 'take it' and 'handle it' were key elements in resisting dominance and asserting equality. This took a particular, racialised, form with Yvette and Natasha, involving dealing with racist behaviour and asserting a specific black identity.

Hayley and Rebecca had explicitly anti-racist views. In Rebecca's case, it seems that her parents had been an influential source. Both girls referred to arriving at their own interpretations, drawing on their own experiences. It was at the level of interpersonal interaction rather than that of their general attitudes to 'race' that contradictory elements emerged. One was the temptation, particularly for Hayley, to use racist name-calling as an instrumental strategy in situations of conflict with Yvette or Natasha. The other was to interpret the assertion of black identity as a dominance-strategy in the group, and react against it. The danger is that the combination of these two social processes could break apart the fragile equilibrium of their interrelationships which they work to maintain and repair in their everyday interaction. That risk may increase as they move into the powerful cultural patterns of adolescence that Hayley and Rebecca describe.

Chapter 10

Conclusions

The schools that we studied are similar to many hundreds of primary schools in urban areas, located in streets of Victorian terraces or new estates on the outskirts. They are similar, too, in containing a minority of black children, perhaps two or three, or half a dozen, in each class. A visitor in the classroom and playground will observe children working together and playing together, black and white, with no sign that 'race' is a significant feature of their lives as children. It is unlikely that such a visitor would overhear a racist remark or witness any other form of racist behaviour. It would be easy to conclude that racism among children is not an issue that such schools need to devote much attention to. These schools seem to confirm the validity of the 'contact hypothesis' that racial prejudice and discriminatory practices are dispelled by the positive experience of white and black children being together in school.

Our evidence does not support this view. On the contrary, it reveals that 'race', and racism, are significant features of the cultures of children in predominantly white primary schools. By far the most common expression of racism is through racist name-calling. There is a wide variation in black children's experiences of racist name-calling. For some it may be almost an everyday happening. For others it is less frequent, with occurrences remembered as significant events whose recurrence remains a possibility in every new social situation. For all, it is in general the most hurtful form of verbal aggression from other children.

The variation in the experiences of black children are not explicable in terms of differences of ethnic group, or of gender. Differences between schools seem to be mainly the consequence of the effectiveness of the stance that teachers, non-teaching staff, and in particular the headteacher, take towards racist incidents, But there is also a wide variation in the experiences of black children in the same school, which is mainly a function of differences in the characteristic patterns of social interaction that black children are involved in, and in particular the level of conflict within them.

Many black children also have experiences of racism outside school. In some cases these are of harassment by other, perhaps older, children. School policies on racist behaviour may suppress it within the school but have no effect on the behaviour of some of the white pupils once they leave the school premises. In addition, many black children have experiences of racism in the adult world: disputes with neighbours, arguments in shops, conflict in the community. These experiences, and the roles taken up by black adults within them, provide a context for their experiences in school, their understanding of them and their responses to them, that other children, and school staff, may be unaware of.

A central objective of this book has been to explore the antecedents, nature and range of race-related incidents in primary schools where there are relatively few black children. Our theoretical starting point was that racist ideologies are not passively received but are used in ways which help children make sense of their material and cultural circumstances. It does not automatically follow, then, that the expression of racism in the parental or school culture, in the media or friendship group, will result in individual children articulating similar convictions. Racism has conditional status in people's lives; conditional, that is, on the extent to which it can be used to make sense of their world. On this view, racism does not exist in isolation, it is relational. It articulates in complex, sometimes contradictory ways with other elements of children's common-sense understandings of their lives. The intricate web of social relations in which children live their lives and the particular set of material and cultural circumstances in which this is embedded have the potential to heighten the salience of racism as an appealing and plausible explanation for 'the way things are'.

The experience for white children of being in everyday contact with black youngsters generates contradictory dynamics, towards racial equality and the de-racialisation of relationships, but also towards the racialisation of existing social processes within children's cultures. In particular, racist name-calling is an important strategy within many children's interaction repertoires (though not in others'), and consequently one that all children have to take up a position in relation to. The meaning of this and other forms of racist behaviour can only be understood in the context of children's cultures, relationships and processes of social interaction.

Children's cultures can be analysed in terms of the interplay of processes of domination and equality. Elements of elaborated and common-sense ideologies, both racist and anti-racist, deriving from family, television and community, enter into and circulate within children's cultures. Here they interact with common-sense understandings generated by everyday social interaction among children. Social processes of dominance and conflict may become racialised in various ways to legitimise forms of racist behaviour. But interaction among children also gives rise to a strong egalitarian dynamic, which may be generalised to issues of 'race' and link up with anti-racist ideologies. Relationships of friendship between white and black children reinforce this egalitarian dynamic, but do not necessarily lead to its generalisation to all black children.

There is a wide variation among white children in their knowledge, attitudes and beliefs about 'race', both within children's culture and in the wider society. Some children are largely ignorant of processes of racial discrimination in society, but the majority of white children have quite an extensive knowledge base and set of interpretive frameworks through which they make sense of issues such as immigration, racial violence, South Africa, and relations between black and white people in their own community. The principal sources outside the school are parents and other adult relatives, television, and their direct experiences in the community. These make available a range of contradictory messages about 'race', and in any case children do not passively receive them but actively select and reinterpret.

The attitudes and beliefs of white children range from those who make use of racist frameworks of interpretation to those who are committed to well-developed notions of racial equality. Many children display inconsistent and contradictory repertoires of attitudes, containing both elements of racially egalitarian ideologies and elements of racist ideologies. The relationship between what we have called children's 'thematic' and 'interactional' ideologies of 'race' is not necessarily one of simple and direct correspondence. On the contrary, interactional ideologies have their own logic, which may be more, or less, congruent with children's 'thematic' attitudes and beliefs. In other words, a number of combinations of attitudes and behaviour is possible, ranging from children who hold racist beliefs but do not express them in behaviour, to children who hold racially egalitarian beliefs but use racist name-calling in certain situations. It follows that racist incidents have a variety of social meanings, and the meaning of any specific instance can only be determined by an analysis of the underlying social processes that produced it.

Within children's cultures, it is primarily interactional ideologies that animate racist ideologies and translate them into social practice. This is clearly the case with interactional ideologies of dominance, which can harness elements of racist ideologies in order to exert power over black children. But racist ideologies can also colonise interactional ideologies of equality. We have described many examples of this: white children using racist name-calling in self-defence; opposing the use of Asian languages on the grounds that it gives an unfair advantage; critical of school policies that seem to privilege the interests of black children. Concepts of equality may serve to justify forms of racial discrimination.

However, our findings also reveal strong dynamics of racial egalitarianism within children's cultures. We would account for them in terms of the combination of two factors. One is a growing awareness of the significance of racial discrimination in society, and its injustice. The other is the development of relationships among children on a basis of equality of treatment and an ability to take and value the viewpoints of others. The growing salience of these two factors during the junior school years may account for the relative decline of racist name-calling during this period that many children referred to. These processes can, however, be overridden and reversed during this period of adolescence by the emergence of powerful peer sub-cultures based on racist interpretive frameworks and interactional repertoires.

WHAT SCHOOLS CAN DO

The first step is to recognise that racism is an important issue for predominantly white primary schools. It has implications for their pastoral and disciplinary procedures and for the curriculum.

The evidence from our three schools is that a clear stance by the school against racist name-calling can be effective in reducing its incidence. Such a policy is welcomed by black children and approved of by almost all white children. The policy at Greenshire school in particular illustrated a number of features which contributed to a reduction in racist behaviour. The policy was well-known to all the children, as a result of statements by the headteacher in assembly and the firm action that she took in dealing with incidents that occurred. There was a clear system of escalating responses by the school, progressing from warnings to the threat of exclusion from the school. Parents were involved if there were repeated breaches of the school policy. In addition, the style adopted by the headteacher in dealing with incidents, combining firmness with a willingness to listen, was appreciated by the children.

There were, however, problems with the stances that all three schools took. For black children, the main problem was that such policies were not implemented effectively by many of the teachers, and also by classroom assistants and lunchtime supervisors. In all three schools the implementation of the policy relied very largely on the headteacher. Many black children saw this as evidence that other staff did not share the headteacher's commitment to the policy. This was reinforced by their experiences of having complained about racist incidents and finding that staff would not listen to them, and that sometimes they themselves got into trouble as a result, either for the original incident, or for complaining. Some black children interpreted this as evidence of racial prejudice on the part of some staff.

Black children face a dilemma if they feel that they cannot rely on staff to deal with problems of racist harassment. If the children try to ignore it it may encourage the offender to continue, but if they retaliate they may get into trouble themselves. The dilemma is particularly acute if their parents advise them to retaliate by hitting the offender. (White children also face this dilemma in other contexts, of course.)

The problem posed in relation to white children is this: a school policy may be effective in reducing racist behaviour within the school, but on its own it may do nothing to challenge the roots of racist behaviour in what we have called children's thematic and interactional ideologies. Racist behaviour may be partially suppressed inside the school but only driven outside the school gates. Furthermore, as long as the underlying roots of racist behaviour remain unchallenged, the existence of a school policy against racist behaviour may be seen as unfairly privileging black children and actually serve to reinforce racist ideas. It is clear therefore that a policy to deal with racist incidents has to be accompanied by a policy for dealing with issues of 'race' within the curriculum.

We have already voiced our scepticism about the efficacy of multicultural education as a strategy through which racism and racist incidents in schools might be tackled. Yet it remains a popular interventionist approach. Lord Elton, for instance, in his inquiry into bullying in schools insisted that the specific case of racist harassment might be obviated through the development of a cultural pluralist curriculum:

> We believe that using the curriculum to emphasise the importance of tolerance and respect for other cultures is a . . . productive approach. A variety of subjects can be used to point out the achievements of different cultures. Where possible these achievements should be linked to cultures represented in the school . . .
>
> (Elton, 1989, p. 110)

The teachers' union, AMMA, agrees; however, it recommended intervention at a later stage in children's schooling. In its statement on multicultural and anti-racist education it advised members to ensure that 'pupils learn about the nature and mechanisms of group prejudice . . . in the formal curriculum, probably at secondary level when children are more likely to benefit from the approach of "knowing the enemy" ' (AMMA, 1987, p. 103). Whilst we support the demand for intervention we reject both the implied deference to the idealised conception of primary school children's understanding of race-related matters and the means advocated. Our objections revolve around two concerns. First, both black and white children have reservations about the promotion of ethnic life styles and cultures in the curriculum. Black children feel embarrassed, even stigmatised, in such lessons, and other research studies have highlighted their resentment towards the fossilised, sometimes racist presentations of their cultures in school curricula (Mac an Ghaill, 1988). White children, on the other hand, resent the school's apparent privileging of ethnic minority cultures and, as a corollary, the devaluation of their own. As we saw earlier, this resentment figured strongly in the Macdonald inquiry into the build-up to the murder of Ahmed Iqbal Ullah at Burnage High School. Multicultural education, according to Gus John, a member of the inquiry, implies that white working-class children 'have to pay due deference to the culture of others even before anybody checked out with them what their perception of their own culture actually was' (John, 1990, p. 70). The children in our schools also seemed to be left high and dry on such matters.

Our second reservation focuses on what we see as the illogical use of 'racial' and cultural categories to combat racism. This is both reductionist and is in danger of legitimating 'race' as an organising and differentiating category. Racist incidents in whatever form arise because 'racial' categories are used as a way of understanding and dealing with particular situations. In short, 'racial' categories have certain functional properties. If racist incidents are to be tackled effectively these categories must be replaced with others which offer young people superior and more plausible explanations for the way things are. Educationists who continue to organise children's experiences around 'racial' conceptions of reality are simply tempting fate.

Our study has a number of implications for a more effective approach to dealing with issues of 'race' in the curriculum. The first is the centrality of the personal experience of the child. We have seen how racist name-calling and other forms of racist behaviour are embedded in and mobilised by the typical social processes of children's cultures. We have also seen how children's ideas about 'race' in society are rooted in and confirmed by their own experiences – of going abroad on holiday, of events in the neighbourhood, and so on. In order to respond to the real meanings of 'race' in children's lives, the curriculum needs to open itself up to and engage with the full range of children's experiences. This point needs stressing in the context of a national curriculum the thrust of which is in the opposite direction. The consultative document on the national curriculum (DES, 1988) states that it will ensure:

> that all pupils, regardless of sex, ethnic origin and geographical location, have access to broadly the same good and relevant curriculum and programmes of study, which include the key content, skills and processes which they need to learn and which ensure that the content and teaching of the various elements of the national curriculum bring out their relevance to and links with pupils' own experiences . . .

We share the concerns that Ken Jones expresses about the implications of this passage which are signalled by the conjunction of 'regardless' with 'relevant'.

The curriculum, apparently, will be relevant to everyone, even though it will have no regard to where they live, what sex they are, and what their racial background is: it will be the same for all, and yet relevant to all! There is a striking confidence that the learning programme devised by the curriculum planners will be fully congruent with the experience of students, alongside an equally striking lack of interest in what that experience might. That students differ in what their society has made of them; that the sexual, class or racial prisms through which they view the world affect their attitudes to learning and their conceptions of relevance are not important matters. Because their lives are seen as empty and cultureless, the national curriculum seems all the more unproblematic.

(Jones, 1989, pp. 96–7)

The children's experiences that we have drawn on in this book are of three types. There are the experiences of relationships and social interaction with other children. We have identified some of the typical social processes at work: domination and equality, hierarchies of age, gender relations, making and breaking friends, group inclusion and exclusion, acting tough, being jealous, and so on, as well as 'race'. It is rare that children have the opportunity to discuss these issues in the educational context. Yet there are ways in which teachers can, both directly and indirectly, through stories, drama, photographs and video, help children to develop their understanding of these issues which are so central to their lives.

The second area of children's direct experience is of 'the adult world': the family, the street, the neighbourhood. Of course, these are commonly reflected in the curriculum. But there is a danger that teachers' representations of these areas of experience may selectively filter out what is of concern to the child. We refer to just two examples from our discussions. 'The shop' is a staple item in the primary curriculum. But is it conceptualised in ways which engage with what the local Asian shop means to Simon, Ben and Richard, or is it divested of the social relationships of 'race'? A number of the children talked about issues of crime and violence in the neighbourhood. Adam, for instance, was constructing racist notions of violence and black people out of a combination of his experiences with black children and the attack on his neighbourhood. Will the curriculum help Adam to make a different sense of issues like these?

The other most important source of children's experiences,

including those of 'race', is television. Our point here is simple: what does school do to help children develop their understanding of television – in other words their skills in 'reading' visual media, whether it is the news or *Grange Hill* or *The Bill* or a Schwarzenegger film?

The curriculum needs to not only address the real experience that children bring with them to the classroom, it needs to offer them the conceptual tools to interpret it. There are two related elements in how the children in our study thought about 'race' that are pertinent here.

The first is their limited understanding of notions of social structure. Many had little or no understanding of how 'race' was socially structured by, for example, the economy and the state. This is a symptom of a general absence of political education in the primary curriculum. Yet it is clear from the evidence of children like Charlotte that children of 10 and 11 years are capable of understanding such ideas, even with little help from the curriculum. The consequence of the lack of 'sociological' concepts was that children tended to use concepts derived from their own experiences of interpersonal interaction to explain phenomena at the level of society. So, for example, lacking concepts of ideology based on material interests, many children explained racist behaviour in society in terms of personal motivations of 'jealousy', transferring a concept that was central to experiences of conflict in their own relationships.

The second conceptual limitation concerned the notion of equality that children used. For many children, white and black, this was a powerful principle capable of organising a consistent anti-racist perspective. But for others, it stumbled at the idea that to achieve equality for the unequal may require unequal treatment, particularly if the inequality is not just at the level of interpersonal relations but is socially structured in ways that the child is not aware of. The curriculum can make an important contribution towards helping children to develop the principle of equality that is so important in their personal lives into a more complex and encompassing concept of social justice.

Finally, we want to stress the two strands that run through the culture of children. We have demonstrated how significant racism is in the lives of white children. We have also been made aware of the strength of anti-racist attitudes and behaviour. The frequent presence of racially egalitarian elements in the thinking even of children who engage in racist behaviour is a crucial factor on which teachers can build. In doing so, the existence in every class of children who have a clear anti-racist commitment is potentially the most powerful resource, if they can be helped to gain the confidence, the skills and the knowledge to express it, both in the curriculum and in interpersonal interaction.

In conclusion, we believe that a school policy needs to have three mutually dependent elements:

1 A clear and firm policy to deal with racist incidents when they occur, which is implemented by all staff not just left to the head. This entails listening to and taking seriously the complaints of black children. The policy must combine both firm disciplinary measures, up to and including exclusion, with a willingness to listen to white children and understand the social meanings of racist behaviour within children's cultures.

2 Similar and related policies to deal with other forms of oppressive behaviour. These may be integrated into a more broadly conceived policy and set of practices which convey the school's stance on and commitment to tackling behaviour aimed at the oppression of discernible groups of pupils: black children, girls, children with disabilities, and younger children, in particular.

3 A curriculum, defined in formal and informal terms, that addresses issues of 'race' in association with related forms of inequality and injustice, both within children's cultures and in the wider society. As we have argued before in our analysis of the murder at Burnage High School, anti-racist teaching needs to be about more than 'race' (Troyna and Hatcher, 1991). Anti-racist education, when defined and put into operation in this inclusive way, should facilitate children's recognition that racist behaviour trades on and helps to reinforce much broader patterns of discrimination. On this view, anti-racist education will help to strengthen (and legitimise) the position of anti-racist children, black and white.

Quite simply, whilst the premise of the 'contact hypothesis' continues to attract support as a justification for not adopting an interventionist anti-racist policy stance, our evidence demonstrates that racism in mainly white primary schools is more prevalent, more complex and more entrenched than many educationists care to admit.

References

Aboud, F. (1988) *Children and Prejudice*, Oxford: Basil Blackwell.

Akhtar, S. and Stronach, I. (1986) ' "They Call Me Blacky" ', *Times Educational Supplement*, 19 September, 23.

Alexander, R. (1984) *Primary Teaching*, London: Holt, Rinehart & Winston.

ALTARF (All London Teachers Against Racism and Fascism) (1984) *Challenging Racism*, London: ALTARF.

Allport, G.W. (1954) *The Nature of Prejudice*, Cambridge, Mass.: Addison-Wesley.

AMMA (1987) *Multi-Cultural and Anti-Racist Education Today*, London: AMMA

Back, L. (1991) 'Social Context and Racist Name-Calling: An Ethnographic Perspective on Racist Talk within a South London Adolescent Community', *European Journal of Intercultural Studies* 1 (3), 19–38.

Besag, V. (1989) *Bullies and Victims in Schools*, Milton Keynes: Open University Press.

Bethnal Green and Stepney Trades Council (1978) *Blood on the Streets*, London: Bethnal Green and Stepney Trades Council.

Billig, M. (1988a) 'Prejudice and Tolerance', pp. 100–23 in M. Billig, S. Condor, D. Edwards, M. Gane, D. Middleton and A. Radley (eds), *Ideological Dilemmas*, London: Sage.

——(1988b) 'The Notion of "Prejudice": Some Rhetorical and Ideological Aspects', *Text* 8 (1/2), 91–110.

——and Sabucedo, J. (1990) 'Rhetorical and Ideological Dimensions of Common-Sense', in J. Siegfried (ed.), *The Status of Common Sense in Pyschology*, USA: Ablex.

Bonnerjea, L. and Lawton, J. (1988) *'No Racial Harassment This Week': A Study Undertaken in the London Borough of Brent*, London: PSI Occasional Paper no. 41.

British Broadcasting Corporation (1973) *'Till Death Us Do Part' As Anti-Prejudice Propaganda*, London: BBC.

Carey, S. (1985) ' "I Just Hate 'Em All, That's All" ', *New Society*, 26 July, 123–5.

Carrington, B. and Short, G. (1989) *'Race' and the Primary School*, Windsor: NFER-Nelson.

——and Troyna, B. (eds) (1988) *Children and Controversial Issues*, Lewes: Falmer Press.

Cashmore, E. (1987) *The Logic of Racism*, London: Allen & Unwin.

Clark, K. and Clark, M. (1939) 'The Development of Consciousness of Self and the Emergence of Racial Identification in Negro Preschool Children', *Journal of Social Psychology*, SPSSI Bulletin 10, 591–9.

——(1947) 'Racial Identification and Preference in Negro Children', pp. 169–78 in T.M. Newcomb and E.L. Hartley (eds), *Readings in Social Psychology*, New York: Holt, Rinehart & Winston.

Cochrane, R. and Billig, M. (1984) ' "I'm not National Front Myself, But . . ." ' *New Society* 68 (1121), 255–8.

Coffield, F., Borrill, C. and Marshall, S. (1986) *Growing Up at the Margins*, Milton Keynes: Open University Press.

Cohen, P. (1988) 'The Perversions of Inheritance: Studies in the Making of Multi-Racist Britain', pp. 9–118 in P. Cohen and H. Bains (eds), *Multi-Racist Britain*, London: Macmillan.

——and Bains, H. (1988) (eds) *Multi-Racist Britain*, London: Macmillan.

Cohn, T. (1988) 'Sambo – A Study in Name-Calling' pp. 29–63 in E. Kelly and T. Cohn, *Racism in Schools – New Research Evidence*, Stoke: Trentham Books.

CRE (Commission for Racial Equality) (1987a) *Racial Attacks: A Survey in Eight Areas of Britain*, London: CRE.

——(1987b) *Learning in Terror*, London: Commission for Racial Equality.

Daniel, S. and McGuire, P. (1972) *The Paint House*, Harmondsworth: Penguin.

Davey, A. (1983) *Learning to be Prejudiced*, London: Edward Arnold.

——(1987) 'Insiders, Outsiders and Anomalies: A Reply to Olivia Foster-Carter', *New Community* 13 (3), 477–82.

Denscombe, M., Szulc, H., Patrick, C., and Wood, A. (1986) 'Ethnicity and Friendship: The Contrast Between Sociometric Research and Fieldwork Observation in Primary School Classrooms', *British Educational Research Journal* 12 (3), 221–35.

DES (Department of Education and Science) (1985) *Education for All*, London: HMSO.

——(1988) *Education Reform Act 1988*, London: HMSO.

van Dijk, T. (1983) 'Cognitive and Conversational Strategies in the Expression of Ethnic Prejudice, *Text* 3 (4), 375–404.

——(1987) *Communicating Racism: Ethnic Prejudice in Thought and Talk*, Newbury Park: Sage.

Dzeich, B.W. and Weiner, L. (1984) *The Lecherous Professor: Sexual Harassment on Campus*, Boston: Beacon Press.

Ekblom, P., Simon, F., and Birdi, S. (1988) *Crime and Harassment in Asian-run Small Shops*, London: Home Office Crime Prevention Unit.

Elton, Lord (1989) *Discipline in Schools: Report of the Committee of Enquiry*, London: HMSO.

Emler, N. (1983) 'Approaches to Moral Development', in S. Modgil, C. Modgil and G. Brown (eds), *Jean Piaget: An Interdisciplinary Critique*, London, Routledge & Kegan Paul.

Flew, A. (1989) 'The School Effect: Review', *Ethnic Enterprise*, November/December, 21–2.

Forgacs, D. (ed.) (1988) *A Gramsci Reader*, London: Lawrence & Wishart.

Foster-Carter, O. (1986) 'Insiders, Outsiders and Anomalies: A Review of Studies of Identity', *New Community* 13 (2), 224–34.

Gaine, C. (1987) *No Problem Here: A Pratical Approach to Education and Race in White Schools*, London: Hutchinson.

Gillborn D. (1990) *'Race', Ethnicity and Education*, London: Unwin Hyman.

Gordon, L. (1984) 'Paul Willis – Education, Cultural Production and Social Reproduction', *British Journal of Sociology of Education* 5 (2), 105–16.

Gordon, P. (1986) *Racial Violence and Harassment*, London: Runnymede Trust.

Gloucestershire County Council (1990) *Combating Racial Harassment in Schools and Colleges: Guidelines for Positive Action*, Gloucestershire: Local Education Authority.

Gramsci, A. (1971) *Selections from the Prison Notebooks* (eds Q. Hoare and Nowell-Smith), London: Lawrence & Wishart.

——(1977) *Selections from Political Writings 1910–20* (ed. Q. Hoare), London: Lawrence & Wishart.

Grugeon, E. and Woods, P. (1990) *Educating All: Multicultural Perspectives in the Primary School*, London: Routledge.

Gunter, B. and McAleer, J.L. (1990) *Children and Television: The One-Eyed Monster?*, London: Routledge.

Hall, M.M. (1989) 'The Terrible Lesson of Ahmed's Murder', *Telegraph Weekend Magazine*, 19 November, 16–25.

Hall, S. (1980) 'Teaching Race', *Multiracial Education* 9 (1), 3–13.

——(1988) 'The Toad in the Garden: Thatcherism Among the Theorists', pp. 35–58, in C. Nelson and L. Grossberg (eds), *Marxism and the Interpretation of Culture*, London: Macmillan.

Hammersley, M. and Woods, P. (1984) 'Editors' Introduction', pp. 1–4 in M. Hammersley and P. Woods (eds), *Life in School: The Sociology of Pupil Culture*, Milton Keynes: Open University Press.

——and Atkinson, P. (1989) *Ethnography: Principles in Practice*, London: Routledge.

Hargreaves, A. (1985) 'The Micro-macro Problem in the Sociology of Education', pp. 21–47 in R.G. Burgess (ed.), *Issues in Educational Research*, Lewes: Falmer Press.

Hartmann, P. and Husband, C. (1974) *Racism and the Mass Media*, London: Davis-Poynter.

Henriques, J. (1984) 'Social Pyschology and the Politics of Racism', pp. 60–89 in J. Henriques, W. Holloway, C. Urwin, C. Venn, and V. Walkerdine (eds), *Changing the Subject: Psychology, Social Regulation and Subjectivity*, London: Macmillan.

Her Majesty's Inspectorate (1984) *Race Relations in Schools: A Summary of Discussions at Meetings in Five Local Authorities*, London: DES.

Hewitt, R. (1986) *White Talk, Black Talk*, Cambridge: Cambridge University Press.

——(1989) *A Sociolinguistic View of Urban Adolescent Relations*, Paper presented to the conference on 'Everyday Life, Cultural Production and Race', Institute of Cultural Sociology, University of Copenhagen, 27–28 April.

Hill, D. (1990) 'The Macdonald Report: A Report and Commentary', pp. 95–108 in P. Pumfrey and G. Verma (eds), *Race Relations and Urban Education*, Lewes: Falmer Press.

Holmes, C. (1985) 'The Myth of Fairness: Racial Violence in Britain, 1911–19', *History Today*, October, 41–5.

——(1988) *John Bull's Island: Immigration and British Society 1871–1971*, London: Macmillan.

Home Affairs Committee (1986) *Bangladeshis in Britain: Volume 1*, London: HMSO.

——(1989) *Racial Attacks and Harassment: First Report*, London: HMSO.

Home Office (1981) *Racial Attacks*, London: HMSO.

——(1989) *The Response to Racial Attacks and Harassment by the Inter-Departmental Racial Attacks Group*, London: HMSO.

Horowitz, E.L. (1986) 'Development of Attitudes Towards Negroes', pp. 111–20 in H. Proshansky and B. Seidenberg (eds), *Basic Studies in Social Psychology*, New York: Holt, Rinehart & Winston.

Humphries, S. (1981) *Hooligans or Rebels? An Oral History of Childhood and Youth*, Oxford: Basil Blackwell.

Husband, C. (1975) 'Racism in Society and the Mass Media: A Critical Interaction', pp. 15–38 in C. Husband (ed.), *White Media and Black Britain*, London: Arrow.

Husbands, C.T. (1983) *Racial Exclusionism and the City: The Urban Support of the National Front*, London: Allen & Unwin.

——(1989) 'Racial Attacks: The Persistence of Racial Harassment in British Cities', pp. 91–117 in T. Kushner and K. Lunn (eds), *Traditions of Intolerance*, Manchester: Manchester University Press.

Jelinek, M. and Brittan, E. (1975) 'Multiracial Education: (1) Inter-Ethnic Friendship Patterns', *Educational Research* 18 (1), 44–53.

John, G. (1990) 'Taking Sides: Objectives and Strategies in the Development of Anti-Racist Work in Britain', pp. 68–71 in *London 2000*, London: Equal Opportunities Unit.

Jones, K. (1989) *Right Turn*, London: Hutchinson.

Jones, S. (1988) *White Youth, Black Culture*, Basingstoke: Macmillan.

Joseph, Sir Keith (1985) 'Without Prejudice: Education for an Ethnically Mixed Society' (Unpublished).

Joshua, H., Wallace, T., and Booth, H. (1983) *To Ride the Storm*, London: Heinemann Education Books.

Kawwa, T. (1968) 'Three Sociometric Studies of Ethnic Relations in London Schools', *Race* 10, 173–80.

Kelly, E. (1988) 'Pupils, Racial Groups and Behaviour in Schools', pp. 5–28 in E. Kelly and T. Cohn, *Racism in Schools – New Research Evidence*, Stoke: Trentham Books.

——(1990) 'Use and Abuse of Racial Language in Secondary Schools', pp. 77–94 in P.D. Pumfrey and G.K. Verma (eds), *Race Relations and Urban Education*, Lewes: Falmer Press.

Kitwood, T. and Borrill, C. (1980) 'The Significance of Schooling for an Ethnic Minority', *Oxford Review of Education* 6 (3), 241–52.

Kohlberg, L. (1976) 'Moral Stages and Moralization: The Cognitive-Developmental Approach', in T. Lickona (ed.), *Moral Development and Behaviour*, New York: Holt, Rinehart & Winston.

Kutnick, P. (1988) *Relationships in the Primary School Classroom*, London: Paul Chapman.

Lasker, B. (1929) *Race Attitudes in Children*, New York: Greenwood Press.

Leahy, R. (ed.) (1983) *The Child's Construction of Social Inequality*, New York: Academic Press.

Mac an Ghaill, M. (1988) *Young, Gifted and Black*, Milton Keynes: Open University Press.

Macdonald, I., Bhavnani, T., Khan, L., and John, G. (1989) *Murder in the Playground: The Report of the Macdonald Inquiry into Racism and Racial Violence in Manchester Schools*, London: Longsight Press.

Marland M. (1987) 'The Education of and for a Multi-Racial and Multi-Lingual Society: Research Needs Post-Swann', *Educational Research* 29 (2), 116–29.

Menter, I. (1989) ' "They're too Young to Notice": Young Children and Racism', pp. 91–104 in G. Barrett (ed.) *Disaffection from School? The Early Years*, Lewes: Falmer Press.

Miles, R. (1988) 'Racialization', pp. 246–7 in E. Cashmore (ed.), *Dictionary of Race and Ethnic Relations*, 2nd edn, London: Routledge.

——(1989) *Racism*, London: Routledge.

Milner, D. (1975) *Children and Race*, Harmondsworth: Penguin.

——(1983) *Children and Race: Ten Years On*, London: Ward Lock Educational.

Modgil, S., Modgil, C., and Brown, G. (eds) (1983) *Jean Piaget: An Interdisciplinary Critique*, London: Routledge & Kegan Paul.

Mould, W. (1987) 'The Swann Report: An LEA Response', pp. 44–60 in T.S. Chivers (ed.), *Race and Culture in Education: Issues Arising from the Swann Committee Report*, Windsor: NFER-Nelson.

Murdock, G. and Troyna, B. (1981) 'Recruiting Racists', *Youth in Society* 60, 13–15.

National Union of Teachers (1981) *Combating Racism in Schools*, London: NUT.

Olneck, M. (1990) 'The Recurring Dream: Symbolism and Ideology in Intercultural and Multicultural Education', *American Journal of Education*, February, 147–74.

Pagelow, M. (1979) 'Research on Woman Battering', pp. 334–49 in J. Fleming (ed.), *Stopping Wife Abuse*, Garden City: Anchor Press.

Phizacklea, A. and Miles, R. (1980) *Labour and Racism*, London: Routledge & Kegan Paul.

Piaget, J. (1932) *The Moral Judgement of the Child*, New York: Free Press.

Pollard, A. (1985) *The Social World of the Primary School*, London: Holt, Rinehart & Winston.

Reeves, F. (1983) *British Racial Discourse*, Cambridge: Cambridge University Press.

Reicher, S. (1986) 'Contact, Action and Racialisation: Some British Evidence', pp. 152–68 in M. Hewstone and R. Brown (eds), *Contact and Conflict in Intergroup Encounters*, Oxford: Basil Blackwell.

Samuel, R. (1989) 'Introduction: "The Little Platoons" ', pp. ix–xxxix in

R. Samuel (ed.), *Patriotism: The Making and Unmaking of British National Identity: Volume II: Minorities and Outsiders*, London: Routledge.

Sihera, E. (1988) ' "The Trouble With You People" ', *Times Educational Supplement*, 16 September, 29.

Smith, D. and Tomlinson, S. (1989) *The School Effect*, London: Policy Studies Institute.

Stone, M. (1981) *The Education of the Black Child in Britain*, London: Fontana.

Taylor, S. (1982) *The National Front in English Politics*, London: Macmillan.

Tattum, D.P. and Lane, D.A. (eds) (1988) *Bullying in Schools*, Stoke: Trentham Books.

Tebbit, N. (1990) 'Salman Rushdie', *The Independent Magazine*, 8 September, 54.

Therborn, G. (1980) *The Ideology of Power and the Power of Ideology*, London: Verso.

Thomas, K. (1984) 'Intercultural Relations in the Classroom', pp. 57–78 in M. Craft (ed.), *Education and Cultural Pluralism*, Lewes: Falmer Press.

Tomlinson, S. (1983) *Ethnic Minorities in British Schools*, London: Heinemann.

Troyna, B. (1981) *Public Awareness and the Media: A Study of Reporting on Race*, London: CRE.

——and Carrington, B. (1989) ' "Whose Side Are We On?" Ethical Dilemmas in Research on "Race" and Education', pp. 205–23 in R. Burgess (ed.), *The Ethics of Educational Research*, Lewes: Falmer Press.

—— ——(1990) *Education, Racism and Reform*, London: Routledge.

——and Hatcher, R. (1991) 'Racist Incidents in Schools: A Framework for Analysis', *Journal of Education Policy* 6 (1), 17–31.

——and Williams, J. (1986) *Racism, Education and the State*, Beckenham: Croom Helm.

Turner, J. (ed.) (1987) *Rediscovering the Social Group*, Oxford: Basil Blackwell.

Waddington, D., Jones, K., and Critcher, C. (1989) *Flashpoints: Studies in Public Disorder*, London: Routledge.

Walker, J. (1988) *Louts and Legends*, Sydney: Allen & Unwin.

Widgery, D. (1986) *Beating Time*, London: Chatto & Windus.

Woods, P. (ed.) (1980) *Pupil Strategies*, Beckenham: Croom Helm.

——(1983) *Sociology and the School*, London: Routledge & Kegan Paul.

Youniss, J. (1980) *Parents and Peers in Social Development*, Chicago: University of Chicago Press.

——(1983) 'Understanding Differences Within Friendship', in R. Leahy (ed.), *The Child's Construction of Social Inequality*, New York: Academic Press.

Subject index

Name index